PROFILES IN MATHEMATICS

René Descartes

Profiles in Mathematics:

René Descartes

Steven Gimbel

Greensboro, North Carolina

Profiles in Mathematics:

Alan Turing
Rene' Descartes
Carl Friedrich Gauss
Sophie Germain
Pierre de Fermat
Ancient Mathematicians
Women Mathematicians

PROFILES IN MATHEMATICS
RENÉ DESCARTES

Copyright © 2009 By Steven Gimbel

All rights reserved.
This book, or parts thereof, may not be reproduced in any form except by written consent of the publisher. For more information write: Morgan Reynolds Publishing, Inc., 620 South Elm Street, Suite 223 Greensboro, North Carolina 27406 USA

Library of Congress Cataloging-in-Publication Data

Gimbel, Steven, 1968-
  René Descartes / by Steven Gimbel. -- 1st ed.
    p. cm. -- (Profiles in mathematics)
  Includes bibliographical references and index.
  ISBN-13: 978-1-59935-060-8
  ISBN-10: 1-59935-060-2
  1. Descartes, René, 1596-1650. 2. Philosophers--France--Biography.
     I. Title.
  B1873.G56 2008
  194--dc22
  [B]
                                                    2008007534

Printed in the United States of America
First Edition

v

Contents

Introduction 10

Chapter One
"Nourished on Letters" 13

Chapter Two
Reading "The Book of the World" 27

Chapter Three
Living a Dream 42

Chapter Four
Making a Reputation 52

Chapter Five
Creating *The World* 63

Chapter Six
The Big Breakthrough 76

Chapter Seven
Friends and Enemies 87

Chapter Eight
The Certainties of Space and Death 97

Chapter Nine
Shoulders of a Giant 108

Timeline 118

Sources 119

Bibliography 122

Web sites 124

Glossary 125

Index 127

Introduction

Mathematics gives us a powerful way to analyze and try to understand many of the things we observe around us, from the spread of epidemics and the orbit of planets, to grade point averages and the distance between cities. Mathematics also has been used to search for spiritual truth, as well as the more abstract question of what is knowledge itself.

Perhaps the most intriguing question about mathematics is where does it come from? Is it discovered, or is it invented? Does nature order the world by mathematical principles, and the mathematician's job is to uncover this underlying system? Or is mathematics created by mathematicians as developing cultures and technologies require it? This unanswerable question has intrigued mathematicians and scientists for thousands of years and is at the heart of this new series of biographies.

The development of mathematical knowledge has progressed, in fits and starts, for thousands of years. People from various areas and cultures have discovered new mathematical concepts and devised complex systems of algorithms and equations that have both practical and philosophical impact.

To learn more of the history of mathematics is to encounter some of the greatest minds in human history. Regardless of whether they were discoverers or inventors, these fascinating lives are filled with countless memorable stories—stories filled with the same tragedy, triumph, and persistence of genius as that of the world's great writers, artists, and musicians.

Knowledge of Pythagoras, René Descartes, Carl Friedrich Gauss, Sophie Germain, Alan Turing, and others will help to lift mathematics off the page and out of the calculator, and into the minds and imaginations of readers. As mathematics becomes more and more ingrained in our day-to-day lives, awakening students to its history becomes especially important.

Sharon F. Doorasamy
Editor in chief

Editorial Consultant

In his youth, Curt Gabrielson was inspired by reading the biographies of dozens of great mathematicians and scientists. "I was driven to learn math when I was young, because math is the language of physical science," says Curt, who named his dog Archimedes. "I now know also that it stands alone, beautiful and mysterious." He learned the more practical side of mathematics growing up on his family's hog farm in Missouri, designing and building structures, fixing electrical systems and machines, and planning for the yearly crops.

After earning a BS in physics from MIT and working at the San Francisco Exploratorium for several years, Curt spent two years in China teaching English, science, and math, and two years in Timor-Leste, one of the world's newest democracies, helping to create the first physics department at the country's National University, as well as a national teacher-training program. In 1997, he spearheaded the Watsonville Science Workshop in northern California, which has earned him recognition from the U.S. Congress, the California State Assembly, and the national Association of Mexican American educators. Mathematics instruction at the Workshop includes games, puzzles, geometric construction, and abacuses.

Curt Gabrielson is the author of several journal articles, as well as the book *Stomp Rockets, Catapults, and Kaleidoscopes: 30+ Amazing Science Projects You Can Build for Less than $1*.

René Descartes

one
"Nourished on Letters"

It seemed so complicated. René Descartes marveled as he looked up from his bed, watching the path of a fly in the late-morning light. The fly buzzed around in seemingly random curves that twisted this way and then that way. Descartes loved geometry, but he quickly grasped that the geometry he had learned in school—the geometry of Euclid—could never describe anything like the path of a fly. Euclidean geometry could manage only problems involving straight lines, circles, and simple curves. To be useful in explaining the real world, Descartes realized, mathematics had to deal with much more complex situations.

As he stared at the fly and the tiled ceiling above, Descartes got an idea. At any given moment, he could assign the location of the fly a numerical "address." All he had to do was start at a corner and count the number of tiles up and the number of tiles over to the fly. A single pair of numbers was sufficient

Profiles in Mathematics

Euclid

to fix the fly's location. As the fly moved, each new location would correspond to a different pair of numbers. Thus it was possible to describe precisely the fly's complicated path as a sequence of changing pairs of numbers, and numbers that change can be discussed in terms of equations. Suddenly what had been a problem in geometry—and one that was too intricate to solve with Euclid's theorems—became a problem that could be solved through algebra.

This ability to translate problems back and forth between the languages of geometry and algebra—what would be called "analytic geometry"—was one of René Descartes' many important contributions to modern mathematics. It opened the door to exact mathematical solutions to problems in physics, chemistry, and biology. Descartes' work changed the course of mathematics and the sciences, but his reach was even greater. His work in those disciplines was embedded in a larger system of philosophy,

René Descartes

a field that Descartes would revolutionize. In short, the complete intellectual landscape looked very different as a result of René Descartes' life.

The story of how Descartes discovered analytic geometry by observing a fly on a tiled ceiling has long been told, though today many historians doubt its accuracy. But the tale does illustrate several important aspects of Descartes' life and work: he was in the habit of remaining in bed, deep in contemplation, until late in the morning. He loved geometry deeply and hoped that all problems could be solved by logical methods of reasoning like those used by geometers. Most of all, he wanted certainty, the search for which became his lifelong pursuit.

Descartes' own story, however, begins in a cloud of uncertainty. He always tried to keep the date of his birth a secret, to prevent anyone from working up his horoscope (a practice that was condemned by the Roman Catholic Church). But the Latin edition of Descartes' book *Geometry*, published in 1649, contains an engraved portrait that includes the author's birthday: March 31, 1596.

The location of Descartes' birth is a different matter still. Most accounts have him born in his grandmother's house near the town of La Haye in Touraine, France. Some sources insist that his mother did not make it to the house but gave birth near a roadside ditch in the neighboring province of Poitou. Both regions continue to claim the honor of being the birthplace of one of France's most celebrated thinkers.

What is known for certain is that René was the third surviving child of his father, Joachim Descartes, and his mother, Jeanne Brochard. His brother, Pierre, was four years older than René; his sister, Jeanne, three years older. Soon after

Profiles in Mathematics

René's birth, his mother became pregnant again, but this time the baby was stillborn. Complications from that birth claimed Descartes' mother three days later, on May 16, 1597. René was only fourteen months old, so he grew up with no memory of his mother.

Descartes' father was not a nobleman by birth. However, like his own father, he had risen to a position of respect and wealth as a lawyer. He had secured a royal appointment as a councilor in the parlement (parliament) of Brittany. Unlike modern parliaments, this was not a lawmaking body but instead implemented royal decrees. Joachim Descartes' position as councilor took him to the regional capital Rennes, far from the family estate in Châtellerault, for six months at a time.

With neither parent around, the care of young René was entrusted to a wet nurse. While he never developed a close relationship with his father, René came to adore his nurse. A deeply religious woman, she would tell him stories about God and heaven. He wanted to believe the stories—a religious urge that would remain with him his entire life—but he demanded to be given explanations for everything. His curiosity was boundless.

René's active mind was not matched by a healthy body, however. His mother had been ill with a lung ailment, most likely tuberculosis, at the time of his birth. He probably contracted the disease from her as a newborn. "I inherited from [my mother] a dry cough and a pale complexion which stayed with me until I was more than twenty," Descartes would later write, "so that all the doctors who saw me up to that time condemned me to die young."

Because of his ill health, René was not sent to school at the same age as most children. Instead, his young mind was

René Descartes

cultivated by his maternal grandmother, who taught him to read and write. He loved books and showed a great intellectual capacity from a very early age. His father—a more practical man who hoped his sons would follow him in society—once quipped that, like expensive books, his younger son was "good for nothing except getting himself bound in leather."

René spent his early years at Châtellerault and his grandmother's estate in nearby La Haye. It was during this period that he first came to know love. "When I was a child," he recalled many years later, "I was in love with a girl of my own age who was slightly cross-eyed; because of this, whenever I looked at her unfocused eyes, the impression which the sight produced on my brain was so joined to that which awakened the passion of love, that for a long time afterward, whenever I saw cross-eyed people, I felt more inclined to love them than others, simply because they had this fault; and yet I didn't know the reason."

René's love for the girl and his predisposition to look kindly upon those whose eyes crossed may have faded as he got older, but what remained with him were questions about perception and thought. How does what we see influence what we think?

These were questions of science and philosophy, and it was not until René went to school that he had the chance to study the answers. Unfortunately, he was not impressed with what he learned.

In 1607, when René was ten years old, he was ready to be sent away for school. However, he was too sick to go in the fall and had to wait until the Easter semester. His father then sent him to join his brother, Pierre, at the newly opened

Profiles in Mathematics

Collège Henri IV at La Flèche. Run by the Jesuits, an order of Roman Catholic priests, La Flèche was among the best educational institutions in all of Europe.

The rector of the school was a Jesuit named Father Etienne Charlet. Quickly recognizing René's superior intellectual gifts, Father Charlet took a personal interest in the boy's education. The relationship between the two would remain close for the rest of their lives. René said that Father Charlet "acted like a father to me during all of my youth."

The days at La Flèche were highly structured according to the standard Jesuit curriculum. Students rose to pray at five o'clock in the morning and had classes from half past seven until it was time for Mass at ten. There was a time for tutoring from noon until two, and a second round of lessons from two until five.

Collège Henri IV at La Flèche in 1655

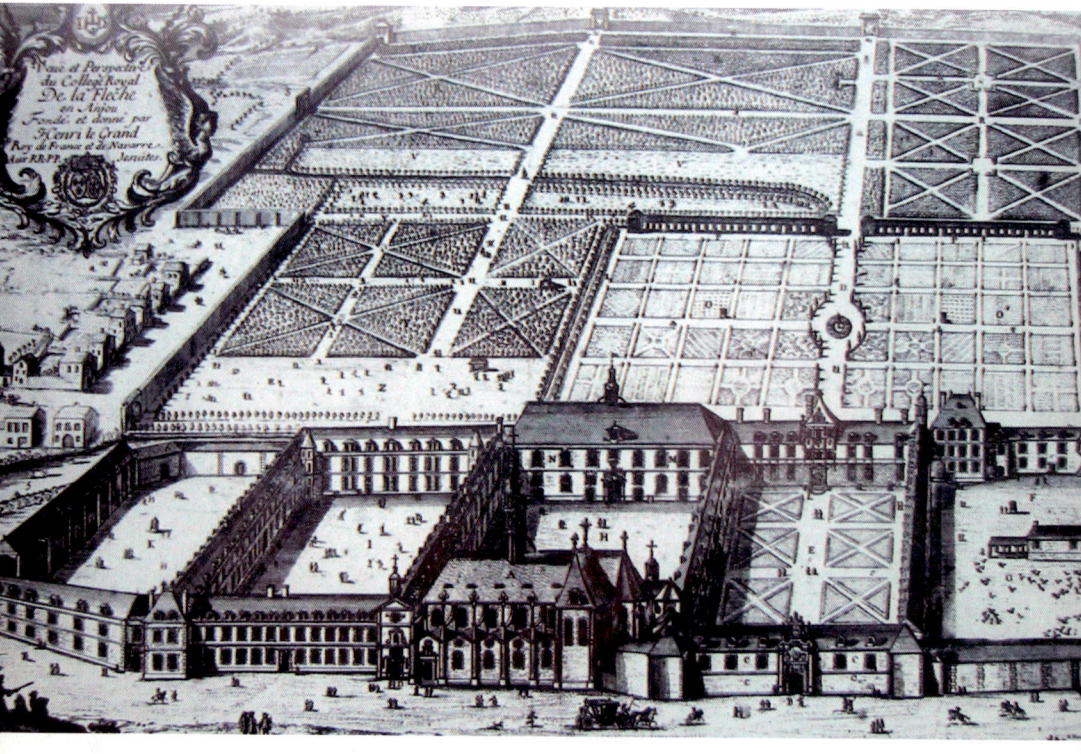

René Descartes

But René's day was different. Father Charlet allowed him to skip prayer, the first lesson, and Mass because he was such a superior student. In addition, the standard treatment at the time for René's constant lung ailment was to lie perfectly still in a well-ventilated room. The fresh air, it was believed, would help clear the lungs. René would therefore remain in bed, alone and still, in contemplative thought until lunchtime. This was a routine he would maintain for the rest of his life. It was during one morning's contemplation that Descartes is said to have observed the fly on his tiled ceiling and gotten the idea for analytic geometry.

During his time at the college in La Flèche, René studied Catholic theology (especially Saint Ignatius of Loyola and Saint Thomas Aquinas), Latin and Greek grammar, classical literature (including Cicero, Virgil, Ovid, Horace, and Seneca), philosophy (Plato, Aristotle, Quintilian, and Demosthenes), mathematics (including Euclid's *Elements*), and science (including physics, astronomy, optics, and acoustics). Indeed, the library at the college was one of the finest in the world, especially in terms of its scientific holdings. René used the library to its fullest, studying widely and acquainting himself with a broad swath

Saint Thomas Aquinas

Aristotle

René Descartes

of classical thought, including writings on forbidden topics such as astrology, alchemy, and magic (writings that were off limits for his classmates).

René remained at the school until 1615. He graduated at nineteen, having completed not only the usual academic track but also an additional course of study in philosophy that was generally reserved for those seeking to become a priest in the Jesuit order. These post-graduate studies in philosophy took three years. In the first year, the concentration was on logic. The second year focused on mathematics and physics. The final year was reserved for studies in what is called metaphysics. Metaphysical questions are what people generally think of when they think of philosophy. They are questions about the underlying nature of reality, such as whether humans have free will or whether their actions are predetermined; whether God exists and, if so, what the nature of God is; and whether all things are made solely of matter or whether there exist nonmaterial entities like souls.

The approach that Descartes' teachers took in exploring these questions, as well as those of logic and the sciences, came largely from the writings of Aristotle, an ancient Greek philosopher from the fourth century BCE. Although he lived well before Christianity, Aristotle's writings were reinterpreted by Christians, primarily Aquinas, and made official doctrine of the Roman Catholic Church. This reinterpretation of Aristotle's thought was presented to Descartes as if it were undeniable fact.

In the end, even with the extra studies, what Descartes learned at La Flèche failed to impress him.

Descartes around the time he graduated from the college in La Flèche
(Courtesy of Visual Arts Library (London)/Alamy)

> I have been nourished on letters since my childhood, and because I was convinced that by means of them one could acquire a clear and assured knowledge of everything that is useful in life, I had a tremendous desire to master them. But as soon as I had completed this entire course of study, at the end of which one is ordinarily received into the ranks of the learned, I completely changed my mind. For I found myself confounded by so many doubts and errors that it seemed to me that I had not gained any profit from my attempt to teach myself, except that more and more I had discovered my ignorance.

Since early childhood, when he had heard stories of heaven from his nurse, Descartes had been seeking to understand the workings of the world with complete certainty. His education had failed to deliver that certainty. At La Flèche he had read the works of the men considered the greatest minds in history. He had delved into a wide range of disciplines. Yet this had merely led Descartes to more questions and, he believed, to errors in thought.

Descartes had, as he would recall later, "delighted most of all in mathematics because of the certainty and the evidence of its reasonings." Mathematics derived logical proofs from simple, undeniable truths.

Descartes recognized the usefulness of math in the "mechanical arts" (such as metalwork, armaments, and navigation). At this point in his life, however, he "did not yet notice its true use." Only much later would he apply the methods of mathematics in the service of his lifelong quest. On math's solid foundations Descartes would attempt to build a comprehensive and certain explanation of the world.

Profiles in Mathematics

Euclid's *Elements*

During Descartes' time, students of mathematics were taught with a text that had been written nearly 2,000 years earlier: Euclid's *Elements*. A Greek living in Alexandria, Euclid compiled all the mathematical knowledge of the ancient world around 300 BCE. His thirteen-book masterpiece included some work by other mathematicians. But what set *Elements* apart—and made it one of the most influential books in the history of mathematics and science—was its logical structure.

Euclid began by setting out twenty-three definitions, such as "a point is that which has no part," five postulates, and five common notions. The postulates are explicitly geometric propositions:

1) It is possible to draw a straight line from any point to any point.
2) It is possible to take any finite line segment and extend it infinitely in a straight line.
3) Given any point and any length, a circle with the given point as the center and having a radius of the given length can be drawn.
4) All right angles are equal to one another.
5) If a line a intersects two other straight lines, b and c, and if on one side of a, b and c angle in toward each other, then if extended far enough, b and c will eventually intersect.

René Descartes

A section of Euclid's *Elements* on ancient papyrus

The common notions are general mathematical truths:
1) If a=b and a=c, then b=c.
2) If a=b and the same amount is added to a and b, then it is still true that a=b.
3) If a=b and the same amount is subtracted from a and b, then it is still true that a=b.
4) If two shapes can be fitted perfectly on top of each other, then they are the same size.
5) The whole is greater than any of its parts.

Profiles in Mathematics

> From these ten obvious truths, Euclid went on to prove a staggering number of very complex results. He included diagrams, but his proofs in no way required them. Instead, he worked step-by-step so that every new move was either one of the ten postulates and notions or a theorem that was already proven using only the ten postulates and notions. In this way, he showed how all the geometry of plane figures must absolutely and necessarily be true if the self-evident postulates and common notions were true.

two
Reading "The Book of the World"

When he left La Flèche in 1615, nineteen-year-old René Descartes—like college graduates before and since—had to decide what to do with the rest of his life. Despite his great intellect and fine education, his options were somewhat limited.

French society during Descartes' time was defined by a rigid class system. All people fell into one of three classes, or what the French called "estates": the nobility, the clergy, and the common people.

Making up a small minority of the population, the nobility enjoyed high social status and a privileged economic position. Unlike the common people, who were heavily taxed by the king, nobles paid no taxes. Membership in the nobility was passed down from parents to children. A person not born into the nobility had little chance of entering it (although extraordinary service to the king was occasionally rewarded with a noble title).

Profiles in Mathematics

Still, there were a few avenues for economic advancement and upward social mobility among non-nobles. One option was to become a member of the clergy. Priests, monks, and nuns were well respected in French society. While they could not expect to become rich, they at least were generally protected from the extreme poverty that peasants faced. For Descartes, who was highly religious and who had a close connection with his Jesuit teachers, there was reason to consider a life dedicated to the Catholic Church. Ultimately, however, he rejected that option.

Another route for advancement was to enter one of the higher-status professions. While a commoner could never attain the privileged standing of the nobility, certain occupations were accorded greater respect in French society. Unskilled laborers were lower in the social hierarchy than craftsmen, who were lower than merchants. Tax collectors were above merchants but below lawyers.

Descartes' family had achieved prosperity and social status through government service. Many members of the family were tax collectors. Descartes' father and brother both rose even higher, gaining appointment as councilors in the parlement of Brittany. Descartes was expected to follow their path.

Gaining such positions, however, required two things: political connections and a law degree. Descartes had the former through his family, but he lacked a background in legal studies. So, following the expectations of his father, he enrolled in the University of Poitiers to earn a law degree.

Poitiers was the home of his mother's family, and Descartes moved in with his uncle, René Brouchard, while he attended the university. His legal studies apparently did not challenge

René Descartes

A view of Poitiers, France, where Descartes lived while attending law school

or interest Descartes much. Later in life he would write in significant detail about the education he received at La Flèche, but he said nothing at all about his studies at Poitiers. Descartes earned his degree in less than one year, beginning his studies in May 1616 and finishing them in November.

Descartes was now in a position to enter the legal profession, which his father clearly wanted. He could have worked as a lawyer, participated in politics, or sought a teaching post at a university. Little stood in the way of a respectable and comfortable lifestyle. But Descartes had no interest in becoming a lawyer.

For a while, he stayed at his father's estate in Rennes, riding horses and studying fencing. He became quite skilled with a foil (the fencer's sword). Eventually he decided to abandon the countryside for a more exciting life in the city.

Profiles in Mathematics

At the time of her death, Jeanne Descartes had left an inheritance for her children, and her younger son was now old enough to collect his portion. The inheritance would enable Descartes to live comfortably for some time. He decided to see the world before settling into an occupation.

Descartes went to Paris, where he quickly fell in with a group of rowdy young men seeking thrills and adventure. The aspect of this wild and carefree life that appealed most to Descartes was gambling. Games that use cards and dice contain elements of chance, which is precisely why they appeal to gamblers. However, Descartes soon realized that the probabilities associated with the games could be thought of in mathematical terms. He began to think deeply about the underlying

Marin Mersenne *(Courtesy of Mary Evans Picture Library/Alamy)*

René Descartes

mathematics, and he worked out some of the foundations of the theory of probability. In the process, he also became an accomplished gambler.

The company of his rowdy friends soon grew tiresome, however. Descartes decided that his life needed more intellectual stimulation. Fortunately, it was at this time that he met Marin Mersenne, who rekindled Descartes' scholarly interests.

Mersenne was eight years Descartes' elder, although they had attended La Flèche at the same time. There are conflicting accounts about the relationship between the two before their paths crossed in Paris. Some sources claim that Mersenne and Descartes had been friends since their school days. Others insist that because of the age difference, they did not know each other well at La Flèche. Their close friendship as adults, however, is beyond dispute.

After leaving La Flèche, Mersenne had continued his education at the Sorbonne. Located in Paris, the Sorbonne was France's most prestigious university. It was also the seat of

Mersenne Prime Numbers

Descartes' friend Marin Mersenne (1588–1648) is best remembered for his work on prime numbers. A prime number is divisible only by the number itself and 1. A Mersenne number is any number of the form 2^n-1. A Mersenne prime is a Mersenne number that is also a prime number. For example, let n equal the prime number 3. Because $2^3-1 = 7$, and 7 is prime, that means 7 is also a Mersenne prime.

Profiles in Mathematics

It can be proven that a Mersenne number will only be prime if the exponent n is prime. But it is not true that all Mersenne numbers with prime exponents are themselves prime. For example, the Mersenne number that results from using the prime exponent 11 is not itself prime.

Mersenne's name is attached to these numbers because he compiled a list of Mersenne primes with exponents from 1 to 257. Unfortunately, his list contained some errors. He incorrectly included two numbers that are not prime. The larger of the two, $2^{67}-1$, was proved to be non-prime in 1903 by Frank Nelson Cole (it is the product of 193,707,721 and 761,838,257,287). The other, $2^{257}-1$, was proved to be non-prime by D. H. Lehmer in 1931 (although this proof merely showed that some pair of factors must exist but did not produce them). Mersenne also left off his list three numbers that are, in fact, Mersenne primes, $2^{61}-1$, $2^{89}-1$, and $2^{107}-1$.

In the continuing search by mathematicians for larger and larger prime numbers, the largest discovered so far is a Mersenne prime. Utilizing the power of personal computers and the Internet, the Great Internet Mersenne Prime Search (GIMPS) ran a program on a huge number of computers. Volunteers permitted their PCs, when not in use, to be used by GIMPS for calculations. As a result, Curtis Cooper and Steven Boone were able to announce in 2005 that $2^{30,402,457}-1$ is a prime number. Written out, it would be 9,152,052 digits long. A year later, on September 4, 2006, in the same room

René Descartes

> just a few feet away from their last find, Cooper and Boone's team made yet another discovery—the 44th known Mersenne prime, $2^{32,582,657}-1$. The new prime is 650,000 digits larger than their previous record prime.

religious and philosophical orthodoxy. Its professors wielded great power concerning which views could and could not be held without violating church doctrine. Mersenne completed advanced courses of study in philosophy and theology at the Sorbonne. Then he joined the Minims, a religious order whose members devoted themselves to a simple, humble life and to the cultivation of the spirit through prayer. A scholar by nature, Mersenne became a philosopher, scientist, and mathematician. But his greatest contribution to intellectual history was his encouragement of other thinkers. Many of Europe's most prominent scholars corresponded with (and sometimes visited) the Minim friar. With his incisive questions, he helped these scholars refine their ideas. He also kept the thinkers within his circle abreast of what others were working on, thereby creating an intellectual cross-pollination that otherwise would not have occurred.

Descartes' introduction to Mersenne in Paris sparked his renewed interest in intellectual pursuits. He and Mersenne discussed mathematics, philosophy, and science. Once again, Descartes had a desire to find certain knowledge.

However, it soon became clear that Paris was not a good place for him to work. His rowdy comrades continually called on him to join in their carousing. Descartes recognized

Profiles in Mathematics

that to progress in his work, he would have to avoid such distractions.

For a man who wanted peace and quiet, Descartes took what today seems like an odd course of action—he decided to join an army. During the sixteenth century, however, the life of a European soldier included long periods of inactivity. In winter, for example, military campaigns were typically suspended and armies rested until the arrival of spring. Descartes evidently believed that a military career would provide him ample time to think. It would also enable him to study two subjects he had developed an interest in—military architecture and strategy—and possibly to find a respectable career as an officer. Perhaps most important, joining an army would enable him to see the world.

Descartes had not found the answers he sought in all the books he had read. Perhaps, he reasoned, the "book of the world" might contain those answers. "I completely abandoned the study of letters," he recalled. "And resolving to search for no knowledge other than what could be found within myself, or else in the great book of the world, I spent the rest of my youth traveling, seeing courts and armies, mingling with people of diverse temperaments and circumstances, gathering various experiences, testing myself in the encounters that fortune offered me, and everywhere engaging in such reflection upon the things that presented themselves that I was able to derive some profit from them."

In 1618 Descartes traveled to Holland and joined the army of Maurice of Nassau, the Prince of Orange. Maurice was a widely respected military strategist who was leading a rebellion against Spain.

René Descartes

The area that today makes up the countries of Belgium and the Netherlands had come under Spanish rule during the early 1500s. In 1568 the seven northern provinces of this region, which all became Protestant, rebelled. These provinces, the most important of which was Holland, would band together in a confederation known as the United Provinces. However, it would take eighty years before they officially won independence as the Netherlands. Meanwhile, the Catholic provinces in the south (today's Belgium) remained loyal to the Spanish crown.

Maurice of Nassau *(Courtesy of Peter Horree/Alamy)*

Profiles in Mathematics

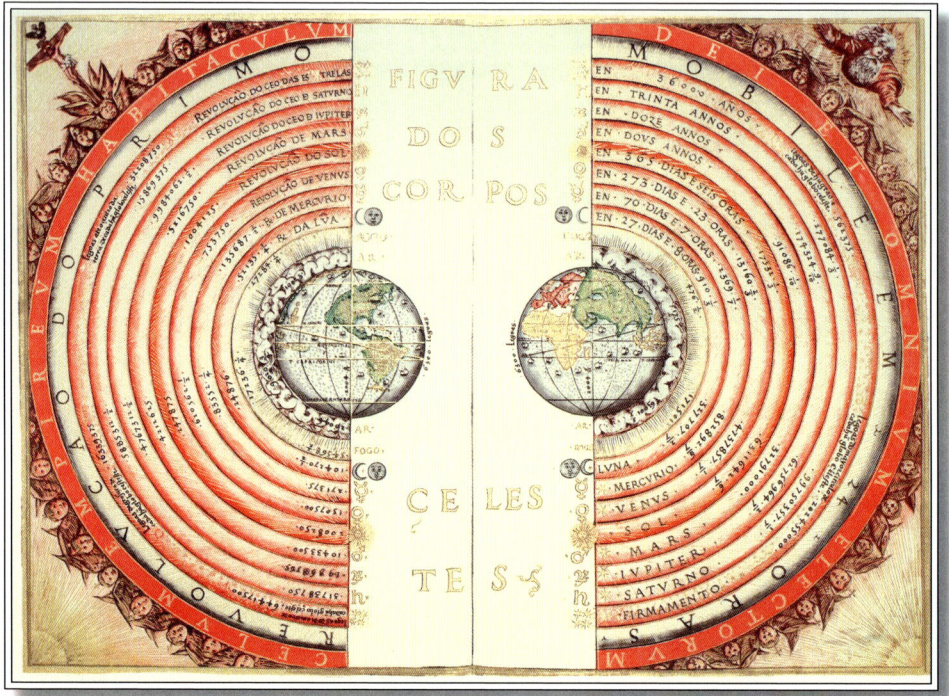

A 1568 illustration of a geocentric solar system

Maurice was leader of the United Provinces. He was also a Protestant. It might seem odd that a devout Catholic like Descartes would fight in a Protestant army. However, the Spanish monarchy was an enemy of France as well.

Fortunately for Descartes, hostilities had temporarily halted when he arrived in Holland. This enabled him to devote time to his intellectual pursuits.

Astronomy was the fashionable scientific topic of the day. The view sanctioned by the Catholic Church came from Aristotle, with later modifications by Ptolemy (ca. 85–ca. 165). Aristotle had placed the earth at the center of the universe, with all other heavenly bodies orbiting around it. Because Aristotle believed stars and planets were more perfect than

René Descartes

terrestrial objects, and because he considered the circle the perfect form, he insisted that the orbits of the heavenly bodies around the earth were completely circular. That assertion did not match astronomical observations, however. Ptolemy, a Greek astronomer and mathematician in Alexandria, modified Aristotle's treatment of the motion of heavenly bodies in a work called *Almagest*. He kept Aristotle's earth-centered universe and circular motions for heavenly bodies. But his system added epicycles (smaller loops along the circular orbits of the sun, moon, and planets) and ecliptics (circles that are off center so that the orbiting body would move faster on some parts of the orbit and slower on others). With these two mathematical techniques, Ptolemy painstakingly arranged circles within circles so that the predicted motion for all the heavenly bodies observable in the ancient night sky perfectly matched observations.

In 1543, however, the Polish astronomer Nicolaus Copernicus published a book in which he put forward an alternative view. The sun, Copernicus said, stands at the center of the universe, and the earth and the other planets revolve around it. The earth, he asserted, also rotates on its own axis as it orbits the sun. However,

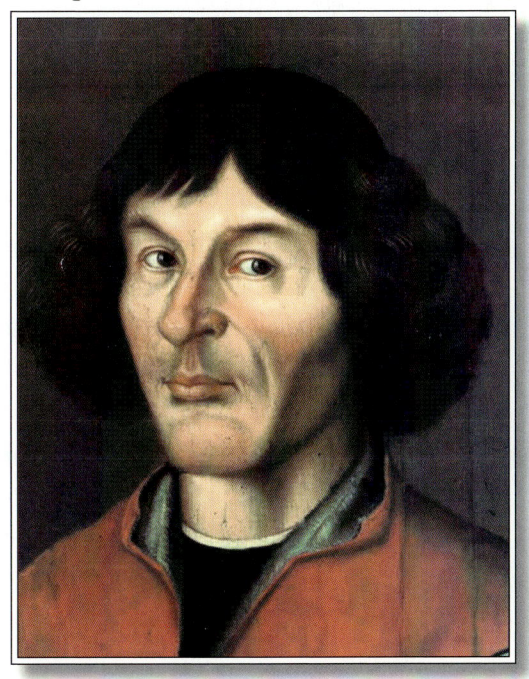

Copernicus

37

Profiles in Mathematics

Copernicus continued to believe the orbits of the planets to be perfect circles, so he continued to make use of epicycles and ecliptics. It was not until 1609 that a German astronomer, Johannes Kepler, correctly stated that the planets' orbits around the sun are elliptical rather than circular.

By Descartes' time the sun-centered view of the universe was gaining adherents throughout the scientific community. Descartes traveled through Germany, Poland, and Holland in search of scientists with whom to discuss the matter.

Ultimately, he wound up in the United Provinces, in the town of Breda. On November 10, 1618, Descartes was walking through town when he came upon a math problem that had been posted as a challenge for the public. This was not an uncommon sight in Dutch towns, as Prince Maurice had a keen interest in mathematics. Because Descartes had been in the United Provinces for less than a year, however, he did not know Dutch well enough to understand what the problem was asking. He asked a passerby to translate the problem into Latin or French. The man did so, and the two struck up a conversation. Descartes' new acquaintance was Isaac Beeckman, a physician with a keen interest in mathematics, science, and philosophy. He was visiting Breda to help his uncle and look for a suitable wife.

Beeckman and Descartes became quick friends. They discussed current research in many areas, including astronomy, geometry, mechanics, and the pressure of liquids. But what drew them together most was their shared belief that scientific problems could be reduced to mathematical problems. At La Flèche, Descartes had been impressed by Euclid's crisp logical method and believed that the certainty he sought might be found by applying this method outside of geometry.

Descartes working at his desk *(Courtesy of Mansell/Time Life Pictures/Getty Images)*

Profiles in Mathematics

Descartes wrote:

> [L]ong chains of utterly simple and easy reasonings that geometers commonly use to arrive at their most difficult demonstrations, had given me occasion to imagine that all the things that can fall within human knowledge follow from one another in the same way, and that, provided only that one abstain from accepting any of them as true that is not true, and that one always adheres to the order one must follow in deducing the ones from the others, there cannot be any that are so remote that they are not eventually reached nor so hidden that they are not discovered.

With Beeckman's help, Descartes began trying to mathematize all the problems of the world. The idea was not simply to copy the method of geometers, but actually to reduce the content of science to mathematics. If this could be accomplished, then Descartes' dream of finding certain knowledge about the world might be realized.

As a start on this project, Descartes wrote his first scholarly work. Called the *Compendium Musicae*, the book dealt with the science of musical harmonies. In it, he sought to give a completely scientific account of music. He related the ratios of the lengths of strings to the pitch they produced when plucked. He then connected this mathematical analysis of musical notes to elements of music theory describing which notes sound good together. In this way Descartes reduced a scientific system, vibrating strings, to mathematical relations. He even showed that human thoughts—in this case, the awareness of beautiful or discordant sounds—could also be reduced. Music became nothing but math.

The human mind, Descartes contended, loves patterns. But at the same time, it can easily be confused by complex relations. Patterns that are not trivial or too difficult to decode, therefore, are the most pleasing. "Among the sense-objects the most agreeable to the soul," he wrote in the *Compendium Musicae*, "is neither that which is perceived most easily nor that which is perceived with the greatest difficulty; it is that which does not quite gratify the natural desire by which the senses are carried to the object, yet is not so complicated that it tires the senses." To study music is to study the mathematical proportions that underlie harmony and tempo. Notes that sound good together bear simple numerical relations to one another (thirds, fourths, and fifths, for example), while certain relations of beats to each measure are also more naturally pleasing to the ear. Those tempos or notes that have no numerical relation or whose ratios are too complex, Descartes said, do not sound good together.

If harmonies could thus be reduced to mathematical form, Descartes believed, so could all other physical systems. And so could human beliefs and emotions. For Descartes, unlike his contemporaries, it was not enough to solve the problem at hand. He had to make the solution general. He had to be able to solve every similar problem.

Descartes dedicated the *Compendium Musicae* to Beeckman and gave him the only copy. He asked Beeckman to keep the book hidden forever in his study because he was sure it contained errors. A close friend could forgive such mistakes, but Descartes did not want the work seen publicly.

While he had taken a bold first step, Descartes realized that his dream of finding mathematical certainty in everything would require much more work. Thanks to Beeckman, however, he was more passionate than ever about the ambitious project.

three
Living a Dream

In 1618, soon after Descartes joined Prince Maurice's United Provinces forces in their fight against Spain, another conflict broke out. It would involve many European states and would rage on until 1648, earning it the name the Thirty Years' War. The struggle would be largely religious, pitting Catholics against Protestants.

Descartes decided to travel to Bavaria and join the army of Maximilian I, the Catholic duke of Bavaria. Maximilian's forces opposed the Protestant army of Prince Maurice, meaning Descartes' former comrades would now be his enemies.

Before beginning his next military stint, however, Descartes decided to travel through more of eastern Europe. He would seek out adventure, spectacle, and great minds in Poland, Denmark, Hungary, and the German-speaking provinces of the Holy Roman Empire.

Descartes ended these travels in Bohemia just as cold weather began setting in. When he assumed his new post as a

René Descartes

Maximilian I

soldier for Maximilian I, negotiations were already under way between the two sides. A truce went into effect, and Descartes spent the entire winter lodged in the comfortable home of one of Maximilian's loyal subjects. Not speaking the language and having no friends or acquaintances there to talk with, Descartes found a delightful solitude "in a stove-heated room, where I was completely free to converse with myself about my thoughts."

The warm, quiet place afforded him the opportunity to concentrate undisturbed.

On November 10, 1619—exactly one year after asking Beeckman to translate the math problem in Breda—Descartes had a series of dreams that changed his life forever. The dreams would spur him to begin working out in detail various elements of the complex project he and Beeckman had envisioned.

Curiously, November 10 has another significance that was familiar to Descartes. It is the eve of the feast day of Martin

Martin of Tours giving half his cloak to a beggar

René Descartes

of Tours, a Catholic saint who lived during the third century BCE. The son of a high-ranking Roman soldier, Martin followed his father into a career in the military, becoming a cavalryman and one of the emperor's bodyguards.

One cold winter day, Martin was fully armed and mounted on horseback when a shabbily clothed beggar approached him. Martin took his cloak—part of his military uniform—and cut it in half with his sword, giving half to the needy man. That night he had a dream in which Jesus, wearing the half of the cloak Martin had given to the beggar, said, "Martin, who is still but a catechumen, clothed me with this robe." (A catechumen is someone who has not yet been baptized.) Awakening from this vision, Martin supposedly found his cloak once again whole. Thereafter he dedicated his life to the Christian Church, ultimately becoming bishop of Tours, the capital of the province in which Descartes was born. As bishop, Martin became famous for destroying many pagan temples and replacing them with churches.

The similarities between own his life and that of Saint Martin were not lost on Descartes: both had ties to Tours, both served in the military, and both had their lives changed by dreams. But Descartes fully expected the story of his dreams to be greeted with skepticism, because the eve of the feast of Saint Martin had another meaning for Frenchmen. It was a holiday marking the conclusion of the harvest, and the French celebrated with food and wine—often a great deal of wine.

For this reason, some scholars have wondered whether the three visions Descartes experienced that night were the result of overindulgence. But Descartes claimed that he had been completely sober that day. In fact, he said, he had not consumed any wine for about three months.

Profiles in Mathematics

Unfortunately, Descartes wrote his only account of the Saint Martin's Eve dreams in a piece entitled *Olympica,* and no copies of that work still exist. However, two scholars who lived not long after Descartes both read the piece and wrote about the dreams described in it. Since these accounts are consistent with each other—one of them even quoting extensively from the now-lost work—it can reasonably be assumed that they are substantially accurate.

The first dream was a nightmare in which evil spirits threatened Descartes as he walked through the streets of a town. Petrified, he struggled to run away as fast as he could. But he found that his right leg would not support him, and he was forced to hobble on his left leg, which guided him to the left, away from the direction he was trying to flee. As Descartes attempted to straighten himself, a great whirlwind took hold of him and spun him around three or four times on his left foot.

Disoriented after his spin, Descartes looked up to see a college in front of him, its gates open. If he reached the college, he thought, he could immediately go to the school's chapel and pray for forgiveness for the sins causing his difficulties. He struggled against the mighty wind. After getting through the front gate of the college, he noticed that he had just passed a man whom he knew. Realizing that he had been very rude in not greeting the man, Descartes labored against the wind to go back and address him properly. But the gale was too strong. It flung Descartes against the outside wall of the chapel.

At this point, Descartes heard the voice of another man calling him by name. The man was extremely friendly and trying to be helpful. As Descartes approached him, the man said that he must go out in search of a Mr. N. He then handed

René Descartes

Descartes a melon grown in another country and instructed him to give the melon to this mysterious Mr. N. Other people soon appeared in the courtyard all around Descartes, who noticed that none of these people were the slightest bit affected by the wind, which continued to toss him about.

Descartes was deeply shaken by this nightmare. Had it been sent by God as punishment for his sins? Was it the work of some evil genius who had figured out how to control his mind? Descartes began to consider the nature of good and evil. After lying awake for a couple of hours contemplating, he once again fell asleep, only to have another dream.

Almost immediately after dozing off, Descartes heard an intense, painful noise like a clap of thunder. Descartes bolted upright in bed and saw sparks of light all around the room. The sparks were so dense that he could only see objects very close to him clearly. Shocked by the vision, not sure at first whether he was awake or asleep, Descartes realized that he had seen such occurrences while awake. Realizing that he was now awake and that the sparks came from the stove, Descartes calmed himself down and once again laid his head down, closing his eyes.

Once more, the Frenchman began to dream. But whereas the other two dreams had been nightmares, the third one was not frightening. Descartes found himself in a room with a table. On the table was a book, but he had no idea who would have placed it there. He went to the table and opened the book to see what it was. When he realized it was a dictionary, he became extremely happy, thinking that it would be of great use to him.

Just then he realized that there was also a second book on the table. He wondered where these books came from. Who

Profiles in Mathematics

could have entered his room and left them? The title of the second book was *A Complete Anthology of the Ancient Latin Poets*. Descartes opened the marvelous volume to a random page and looked at the poem there. The poem's first line read, in Latin, "What path shall I follow in life?"

A stranger suddenly walked into the room and began reciting to Descartes part of a poem in Latin whose first line was "It is and it is not." The man expressed how wonderful the poem was, and Descartes told the stranger that he had studied the poem, instantly recognizing it as a part of the *Idylls* by the poet Ausonius. Descartes realized that the poem was in the book he had just been reading and tried to find it in the large collection. He rifled through pages desperately trying to find the poem, but to no avail.

The man asked him where he had gotten this book. Turning to face the man, Descartes was embarrassed to say that he did not know. He went to look again for the verse, but the volume had disappeared. Frantic, Descartes looked at the table and saw that the book had reappeared on the far side. The dictionary had not moved, but he realized that it was now a different edition. After again futilely trying to locate the poem in question, Descartes told the visitor that he knew an even better poem by the same author. It began, "What path shall I follow in life?" Descartes was sure he would be able to locate that poem in the anthology. He turned to get a response, but the visitor and the book both disappeared, leaving Descartes to ponder the meaning of the episode.

Descartes ultimately took the dreams to mean that he ought to dedicate his life to study. He believed the dictionary in the third dream signified the definitions of science

René Descartes

and philosophy, and the anthology of poems suggested inspiration. His task would be to unite scientific knowledge and the wisdom of the poets into a coherent structure of thought. Only then could certainty in human knowledge be achieved. The phrase "It is and it is not" said to Descartes that within the structure of human belief there is both truth and falsity. If Descartes hoped to find the truth, he would have to begin to think about all human knowledge. He felt sure that what had been revealed to him would turn out to be the foundation for all human sciences. He tried to interpret the other parts of his dreams: the wind, the melon, why his right side would be impaired. All of this led him to his stove-heated room for deep contemplation.

Descartes remained in Maximilian's army after the winter of 1619-1620, though historians disagree in what capacity he served. Some believe that he was a military engineer and did not see any combat. Others suggest that he participated in several engagements and distinguished himself at the Battle of White Mountain, fought near Prague on November 8, 1620. In any case, everyone agrees that his military training ultimately came in handy.

Having decided to return to Paris in order to continue his intellectual pursuits, Descartes was on a boat bound for Holland. He and his valet were the only people on board the ship who spoke French, and they conversed often. The Dutch crew observed the two men and made several assumptions: that Descartes was a wealthy merchant, since he could afford a personal valet; that he would be an easy target, as he was traveling without bodyguards; and that he understood only French. In Dutch, they openly conspired to rob and murder Descartes and throw his body overboard. But

Profiles in Mathematics

The Battle at White Mountain in 1620, fought during the Thirty Years' War. *(Courtesy of Imagno/Austrian Archives/Getty Images)*

Descartes, having lived for a period in the United Provinces, understood what the sailors were planning. Outnumbered, he realized that his best chance lay with the element of surprise. He waited for the proper moment and then pounced on one of the plotting sailors, drawing his sword and raising it to the man's throat. Speaking in Dutch, he told the sailors that he understood every word they had said and would kill them all himself unless they rowed him and his companion without delay to the shore. Shocked at the turn of events, the crew obeyed.

Descartes completed his journey back to France over land. He stopped at Rennes, visiting his father and selling the parcel of land that his mother had left to him. Using the money from this sale, Descartes resumed his travels. This time he was off to Switzerland and Italy. Fortunately, the rest of his travels held less adventure than his boat ride to Holland. Ultimately the path led back to Paris.

four
Making a Reputation

Descartes' return to Paris in the summer of 1625 was a chance to begin his scholarly pursuits in earnest. Marin Mersenne introduced him to the great thinkers of Paris and to the work of intellectuals across Europe. But Descartes retained his old bias from school: he did not think there was much value to be found in other people's writings. "Plato says one thing, Aristotle another, Epicurus another, Telesio, Campanella, Bruno, Basson, Vanini, and the innovators all say something different," Descartes wrote to his friend Isaac Beeckman. "Of all these people, I ask you, who is it who really teaches me, or indeed anyone who loves wisdom?" He would have to discover truths on his own, and his thoughts were always focused on his own project: the search for certainty.

Having taken up residence in the house of a family friend, Monsieur Levasseur d'Étoiles, Descartes spread his time and

René Descartes

effort between problems in philosophy, mathematics, physics, and other sciences. But his main focus was on developing a new method of thought that could underlie his work in all of these areas and guarantee exactitude.

Descartes had become friends with the mathematician and scholar Claude Hardy, who had recently published a new edition of the *Elements,* Euclid's masterwork on geometry, with his own new translation into Latin and explanatory notes to accompany the text. The deep admiration Descartes had acquired for Euclid's work while a schoolboy at La Flèche had been renewed, and the idea that classical geometry should serve as a template for all other sorts of intellectual endeavors led him to begin thinking hard about a universal method.

Descartes working on his universal method of knowledge based on certainty *(Courtesy of The Stapleton Collection/The Bridgeman Art Library)*

Profiles in Mathematics

Descartes was not the only person who was thinking along these lines. A few years earlier, the Englishman Sir Francis Bacon had written a book called *New Organon*, which sought to lay out in clear, simple terms a method by which all investigations of the world should proceed. Descartes was not keen on Bacon's suggestions, though.

For Bacon, thinking must begin with observation. To understand the world, one must first use the senses to collect pieces of information about observable phenomena. From these observations, Bacon argued, emerge patterns and regularities. Science, he said, proceeds when regularities are generalized. If, to use a famous example, every swan that has been observed is white, then one could hypothesize that all swans are white. The more white swans that are seen, the more certain the hypothesis. Finding even one black swan, however, would prove the hypothesis wrong. At that point a search for new patterns and regularities would have to begin. Scientific knowledge, according to Bacon, is always contingent. Through continual observation, scientific theories are refined or

Sir Francis Bacon

René Descartes

rejected. But the whole enterprise must begin with perception, with looking at the world.

For Descartes this was completely unacceptable. Human senses can be fooled, so for this reason Bacon's method could not provide the certainty Descartes sought. But even if the senses were reliable, general statements that went beyond one's own observations would always be open to doubt. Just as the statement "All swans are white" could be disproved by observing black swans in a previously unexplored part of the world, Bacon's method required that any claim be subject to modification as a result of new observations. Such a method could never offer certainty. So Descartes would have to construct a radically different sort of method from a very different starting point.

Nevertheless, Descartes did like aspects of Bacon's work. It was easy to read and easy to use. Bacon had written a manual for the mind that people could actually follow. Descartes would need to do the same thing, only with a methodology he considered proper. Descartes eventually called it *Rules for Guiding One's Intelligence in Searching for the Truth*. It contained three sets of twelve rules. These rules were written out simply and clearly in a way that any educated person could understand. Immediately below the rules were explanations so that anyone could make use of them.

This was not Descartes' only project, however. In his mathematics work, he made a major breakthrough: he solved a problem that had been unsolved since ancient times, the construction of mean proportionals. The problem is this: Take any two line segments with lengths a and b, respectively. What are the other line segments with lengths x and y that

Profiles in Mathematics

are needed in order to make the following proportions true: $a:x = x:y = y:b$? For example, if the first line segment is one inch long and the second line segment is eight inches long, then the mean proportion $x:y$ is 2:4. That is, the two missing segments are of lengths two and four inches because 1:2 as 2:4 as 4:8. This example is easy because these particular values for a and b happen to have a trivially simple solution. But to solve this geometric problem for line segments of arbitrary lengths, the problem was quite difficult—indeed impossible—if approached with merely a straightedge and a compass, as the Greeks had attempted.

Part of Descartes' solution involved using circles and parabolas instead of the lines and circles produced by straightedges and compasses. But another key part required translating the relation between the circles and parabolas into equations and using algebra to get an answer that could then be translated back into geometric terms. Descartes and the mathematician Claude Mydorge produced a proof based on the idea of reducing problems in one part of math to more easily solvable—and, critically, exactly solvable—problems in another part of math. Descartes realized that they had come upon something powerful. Others had arrived at solutions to the problem of mean proportionals that were better or worse approximations. But Descartes declared that his result was among the most important in the history of human thought because he had solved it exactly. He provided a method that yielded a general solution to the whole class of problems, not just a specific instance, and he did it in a fashion that provided absolute certainty. In at least this one place, this one problem, he had found certainty, and he had done it by reducing problems of one sort to problems of another.

René Descartes

While he was doing this work, Descartes also became fascinated by a novelty that was all the rage in Paris: fountains that had moving figures and made music. The statues had pipes running through them that were filled with water. The pressure from the water could be used to move parts of the statue or to make sounds like a calliope. Today such machines would be called "hydraulic," and they have become commonplace. But during Descartes' time they were not only novel, they were revolutionary. Suddenly actions that seemed to require a mind—movement and sound—could be produced by simple physical interactions. If statues could be made to "come to life" in this way, Descartes wondered, maybe all living things were really just like statues. If the seemingly impossible problem of mean proportionals could be solved by reducing it to a question in a different field, maybe the problems of the human body could similarly be reduced to physics and then geometry. Descartes had already shown that he could reduce geometry to algebra, and algebra yielded exact solutions. It was all starting to come together. The method of reduction appeared to offer universal certainty.

While trying to apply this new method to various problems, Descartes tried to work out his thirty-six rules for the method. Despite considerable effort, however, he could not hone the rules to his satisfaction.

During the winter of 1627-1628, Descartes attended a lecture that would change his life. The lecturer, a chemist and medical doctor named Sieur de Chandoux, had been invited to speak before a group of scholars by the papal nuncio, a powerful representative of the pope. The topic of Chandoux's talk—the failings of Aristotle's worldview—was a potential minefield. The Catholic Church had incorporated

Profiles in Mathematics

much Aristotelian philosophy into its official doctrine, and deviation from official doctrine constituted heresy, a crime for which there were terrible punishments. Yet the nuncio's sponsorship of his lecture gave Chandoux a degree of latitude. Chandoux argued that not only were Aristotle's results wrong, his method was faulty as well. The method he suggested allowed that probabilities were necessary. He further proposed that one could only know something to be more or less probably true.

At the end of his daring lecture, Chandoux received a great ovation. Descartes, however, was visibly unenthusiastic. When the papal nuncio noticed this, he asked Descartes what he had not liked about the lecture. At first, Descartes declined to comment. But his powerful host insisted.

Descartes commended Chandoux for his eloquence, his courage, and his forthrightness. But he objected to the idea that absolutely certain knowledge was to be replaced by beliefs with degrees of certainty. Descartes asked audience members for any proposition that they thought true and proceeded to construct plausible arguments that it was false. He then asked for any proposition that someone in the audience thought was false. Again, he gave plausible arguments that showed it was true. If, as Chandoux advocated, there was only *likely truth* and *likely falsity*, a smart enough person could make truth into falsity and falsity into truth. Absolute certainty, and only absolute certainty, was needed—and Descartes thought he knew how to achieve it. Descartes wrote in a letter to Etienne de Villebressieu, who had also attended Chandoux's lecture:

> You saw these two results of my fine Rule or Natural Method in the discussion which was forced on me in the presence of the

René Descartes

> Papal Nuncio, Cardinal de Berulle, Father Mersenne and all that great and learned company assembled at the Nuncio's palace to hear M. de Chandoux lecture about his new philosophy. I made the whole company avow what great power the art of right reasoning has over the minds of those who have no learning beyond the ordinary. I showed them that my principles are more certain, more true and more natural than any of those which are currently received in the learned world.

Clearly, Descartes believed that his performance at the lecture constituted an intellectual tour de force. The papal nuncio apparently agreed. He asked Descartes to pay him a personal visit, during which Descartes described his project and the rules he was working on. The papal nuncio gave him great encouragement, telling him that it was his God-given duty to use the skills of his intellect to their greatest ends. Descartes was now more convinced than ever that he needed to concentrate on his search for certainty.

Unfortunately, his performance at the lecture made that more difficult. His reputation as a first-rate intellectual reinforced, Descartes soon found his once-quiet study swamped with admiring visitors.

Descartes' reputation also gave rise to speculation of a dark sort. He was rumored to be a member of a secret society called the Rosicrucians. Historians are unsure whether this shadowy organization—also known as the Confraternity of the Rose Cross and the Invisible Brotherhood—actually existed during Descartes' time or was merely a hoax. In the seventeenth century, however, the group was widely believed to be real. And some people attributed to the Rosicrucians—whose members supposedly included the most intelligent and learned figures in Europe—satanic powers and menacing

Descartes *(Courtesy of Mary Evans Picture Library/Alamy)*

René Descartes

designs. The Rosicrucians were said to possess powers of magic, the secrets of alchemy, and knowledge of astrology. Their goal, it was said, was to infiltrate politics and surreptitiously gain power with an eye toward restructuring the whole world.

In France—and particularly in Paris—the Rosicrucian scare had taken hold around the time of Descartes' return from eastern Europe. But that was not the only reason some Parisians eyed him with suspicion. Descartes had traveled throughout Germany, where the Invisible Brotherhood was supposedly centered. A leading thinker himself, he had met with prominent intellectuals across Europe—and he made no secret of that fact. It was said that Rosicrucians had to communicate with other Rosicrucians in many or even all of

A Rosicrucian symbol *(Courtesy of Visual Arts Library (London)/Alamy)*

Profiles in Mathematics

the world's tongues, and Descartes was a polyglot. In addition to his native French, he had learned Dutch and German during his travels, and he knew Latin, Greek, and Hebrew from his days as a student at La Flèche.

Descartes had a standard response when suspicious Parisians asked whether he was a Rosicrucian. He could prove with absolute certainty, Descartes claimed, that he was not from the Invisible Brotherhood. Pointing to his body, he would ask his questioner, "Can you see me?"

Despite this sarcastic putdown, the continual queries about Rosicrucianism—along with the nonstop visitors to his study—were an annoyance. Descartes was able to get very little work done in Paris. He knew that he would require vast undisturbed periods of time for contemplation. The search for certainty would first require a search for solitude.

five
Creating The World

Around 1629, Descartes moved back to Holland. There he found the solitude that he so needed to pursue his work. No one bothered him because no one knew him. Descartes reported to a friend in Paris:

> In this great city [Amsterdam], where everyone except me is engaged in business, each is so worried about his own profit that I could remain here my entire life without ever being seen. I go for walks every day in the confusion of great crowds with as much freedom and repose as you would find in your parks; and I consider the men whom I see just like the trees or animals in your forests. Even their noise interrupts my reverie no more than the rustle of a brook.

Still, Descartes went to great lengths to avoid acquiring local acquaintances, who might distract him from his work. He moved continually, living in multiple residences in four

Descartes in Amsterdam *(Courtesy of North Wind Picture Archives/Alamy)*

different cities over the course of three and a half years. He also tried to prevent foreign scholars from visiting him by putting false return addresses on his letters—even those to his dear friend Mersenne.

Descartes made use of his hard-won solitude to renew his quest for certainty. He attacked the project from several directions. He began working on a theory of mechanics (the science of motion) that was radically different from the accepted view of Aristotle. He conducted research in optics (the science of light), working with lenses. He did experiments in human anatomy and physiology to explain why the heart beats, how blood circulates, and how sensations move from sense organs into the mind. In Descartes' view, all of these studies were intimately connected. One could not explain vision, for example, without understanding how light behaves, how the eye functions, and how the mind interacts with the body. Descartes regularly visited the local butcher, taking home various parts of animals, especially the eyes, to carefully dissect and closely observe.

Descartes was seeking to answer specific questions through science, but he was also attempting to construct a strict methodology and logic of science. For Descartes, the how was as important as the what.

Descartes' task was greatly complicated by his religious beliefs. A pious Catholic, he was determined to conform his scientific work to Catholic teachings. Yet science and the Catholic Church seemed to approach knowledge in fundamentally different—and perhaps irreconcilable—ways. In science, observation was the first step in uncovering truths about the workings of the natural world. The Catholic Church, however, had already adopted certain

132　　　LA DIOPTRIQUE

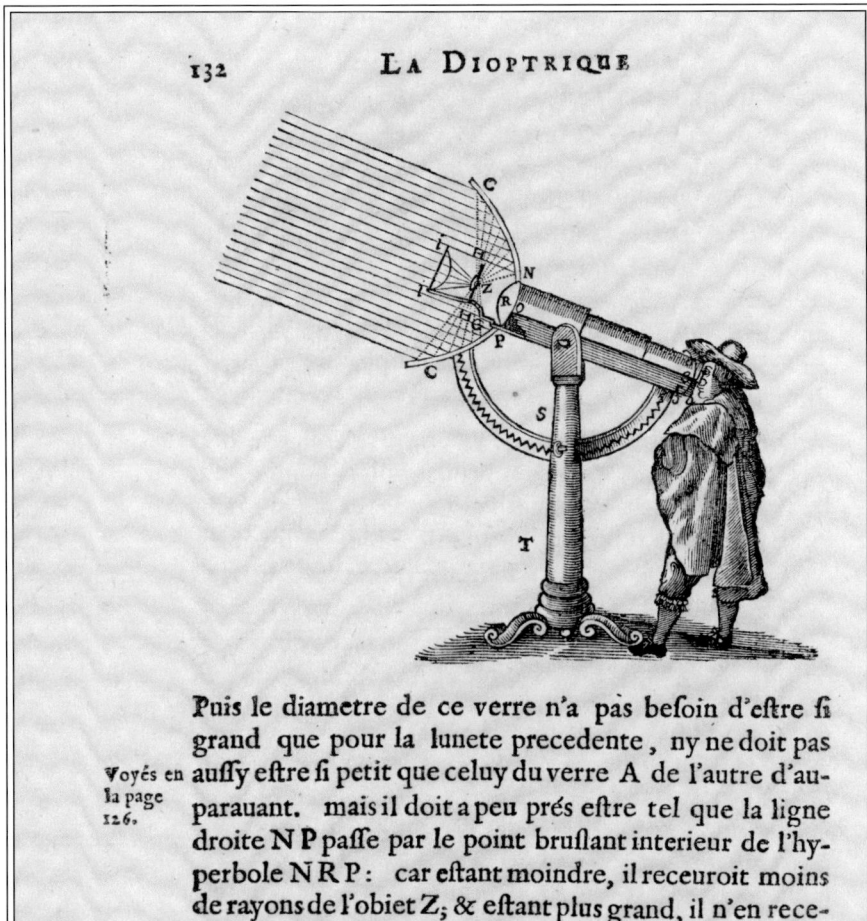

Voyés en
la page
126.

Puis le diametre de ce verre n'a pas besoin d'estre si grand que pour la lunete precedente, ny ne doit pas aussy estre si petit que celuy du verre A de l'autre d'auparauant. mais il doit a peu prés estre tel que la ligne droite N P passe par le point bruslant interieur de l'hyperbole N R P: car estant moindre, il receuroit moins de rayons de l'obiet Z; & estant plus grand, il n'en receuroit que fort peu d'auantage; en sorte que son espaisseur deuant estre a proportion beaucoup plus augmentée qu'auparauant, elle leur osteroit bien autant de leur force que sa grandeur leur en donneroit, & outre cela l'obiet ne pourroit pas estre tant esclairé. Il sera bon aussy de

During Descartes' examination of certainty, he conducted research in optics and lenses. This illustration of a compound microscope is from one of Descartes works. *(Library of Congress)*

René Descartes

explanations of the natural world (largely from Aristotle) as official doctrine. And official doctrine was unquestionable truth. Thus the faithful were expected to accept the received wisdom handed down by the pope and the rest of the church hierarchy. Nevertheless, Descartes committed himself to finding a way to make advances in science and explain how science should proceed, while still not violating his Catholic beliefs.

Descartes mostly maintained his self-imposed social isolation as he contemplated this difficult undertaking. However, there was one person in Holland whose company he sought out: Isaac Beeckman. The two were clearly close friends. Yet Descartes' periodic visits to Beeckman's home in Dordrecht were motivated by more than just friendship. Descartes respected Beeckman's learning, and the two exchanged ideas, worked out problems, and explored new avenues of interest. Descartes especially valued their discussions of geometry and astronomy.

In late 1629, however, the two had a terrible falling-out. The trouble began in the summer, when Marin Mersenne visited Beeckman in Dordrecht. The two talked about musical harmonies, especially the work done by their mutual friend Descartes. In a subsequent letter to Mersenne, Beeckman implied that Descartes—who was seven years his junior—had been his student, not that the two had been collaborators working with Descartes' ideas. When Mersenne mentioned this in a letter to Descartes, the latter became extremely angry. Descartes believed that his trust had been violated. More important, he was being denied his due for his work. Throughout his life, Descartes was always keen to make sure he received full credit for ideas that were his. And here was a

67

Profiles in Mathematics

dear friend trying to claim the glory for work that Descartes had shared in confidence.

In December 1629, Descartes took back the manuscript he had given to Beeckman a decade earlier. The following year, still fuming, he wrote an angry letter. "You prefer stupid boasting," he told Beeckman, "to friendship and truth. . . . If you claim to have taught something to someone, it is repulsive to do so even if you speak the truth; when it is false, however, it is much more repulsive; finally, if you yourself learned it from this person, it is most repulsive."

However, Beeckman continued to characterize Descartes as his student and said to a mutual acquaintance that the younger man would advance much faster in his research if he came back to work with his old teacher. Descartes seethed. The two were no longer on speaking terms, and Descartes said that Beeckman's letters might be useful one day in a book on ethics—to show people how not to act. The quarrel would last another year before the two finally made up.

In that time Descartes continued working. After four years of diligent work in Holland, he finally had something to show: the completed manuscript of a book titled *Le Monde* (*The World*). Sadly, the finished manuscript has not survived. However, it is possible to piece together a fairly comprehensive picture of what it contained, based on an incomplete version found among Descartes' papers after his death as well as correspondence from his years in Holland.

The project was extremely ambitious: it attempted to explain the whole world. Descartes proposed a single, coherent account of all natural phenomena, including the inner workings of humans. "I think that the science I describe," Descartes informed Mersenne, "is beyond the reach of the

René Descartes

human mind; and yet I am so foolish that I cannot help dreaming of it though I know that this will only make me waste my time as it has already done for the last two months."

To add to the complexity of the project, Descartes tried to demonstrate that it did not conflict with his religious beliefs. *The World* was to be no less than a scientific reconstruction of Genesis. Whereas the biblical story set out how the Creation happened theologically, Descartes' version would show how it happened scientifically. Descartes, of course, did not claim to be a prophet. His account was not the result of mystical or divine revelation; quite the contrary, because for Descartes the rational method was every bit as important as the results.

Descartes began by framing his project as a fable. He asked his readers to pretend that God was creating a new universe and they got to watch. He then asked, What would God have to do? What is the smallest number of laws that God would have to use to make the universe run as well as ours? What would those laws be?

By proceeding in this fashion, Descartes derived a new picture of the world that differed in important ways from the account of Aristotle. For Aristotle all objects on or near the earth were composed of a combination of four elements: earth, air, fire, and water. Each element existed in empty space and had a natural place in space where it belonged. All things, because they had a natural place, had an internal desire to seek that place. This, Aristotle said, explains why water moves in a straight line toward the center of the earth and fire moves in a straight line away from it. The water and the fire are both trying to go to their natural resting place in the shortest way possible.

Profiles in Mathematics

Descartes, by contrast, did not believe there were distinct elements with internal desires that existed in empty space. Rather, he said, space is filled at every point with particles whose only properties are their position, shape, and size. The interaction of these particles is what gives rise to all that people see. The different arrangements, motions, and interactions are what give rise to the different states and kinds of matter.

According to Aristotle, things will naturally move if they are someplace other than their natural place of rest. Descartes, on the other hand, proposed what is now called the principle of inertia—that is, objects that are at rest stay at rest unless pushed by something else, and objects that are moving continue to move unless stopped by something else.

Descartes' theory of physics included many other explanations of natural phenomena. These explanations were based on hypothetical laws of nature that God would have used in creating the universe. Most interesting of all was the proposition that the motion of the heavenly bodies was not at all what Aristotle had envisioned. Whereas Aristotle (and Ptolemy after him) had put the earth at the center of the universe, Descartes' universe was Copernican, with the earth and the other planets circling the sun.

Descartes also delved into the nature of human beings. Having done away with internal sources of motion for a more machine-like picture, he was puzzled by problems like the continual beating of the heart. Descartes' solution was to view the human body as a complex machine. Just as people can build moving fountains, so God could make such a "living statue" in an extremely intricate fashion. God was the ultimate engineer and could create amazingly complex versions

René Descartes

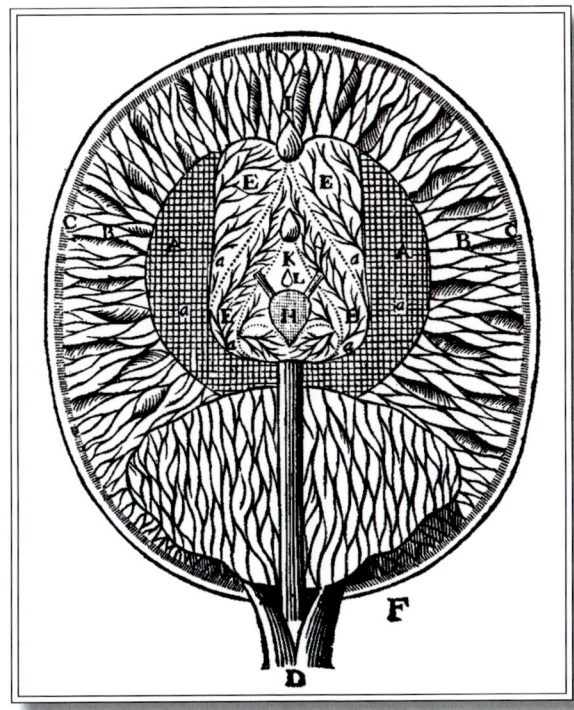

Descartes' diagram of the human brain

of the hydraulic fountains and sculptures that Descartes had seen in Paris. God's statues were human bodies, which would also house a non-material soul.

But if humans were just hydraulic fountains, where in the body were the tubes, and what was the fluid flowing through them? The tubes, Descartes decided, were the arteries and veins. But the fluid that caused the human body to move could not be blood, because blood is itself always moving, even when the body is not. The fluid that caused the body to move was something Descartes called "animal spirits." The animal spirits, Descartes said, circulate through the body with the blood and convey energy to the heart just as a flame heats up an object. The blood "is turned into spirits by the warmth of the heart and travels through the arteries to the brain and from it to the nerves and muscles," Descartes wrote.

But the animal spirits could also be used to explain another problem that Descartes needed to account for: If the mind and the body were two completely different things—as Descartes

Profiles in Mathematics

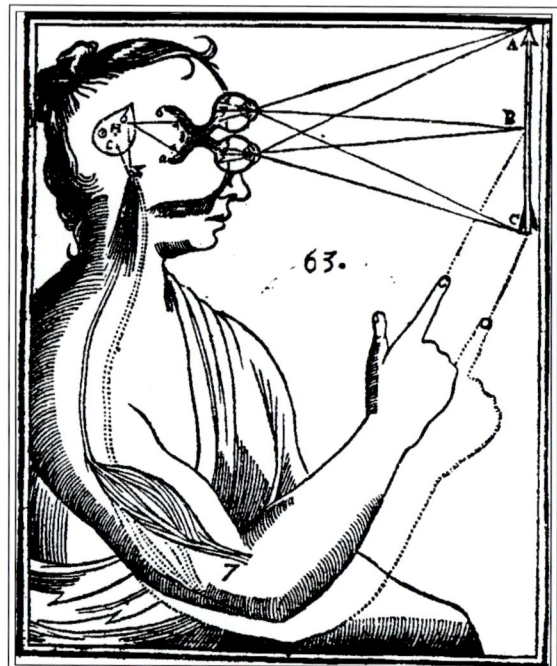

This diagram by Descartes attempts to explain how the brain receives and processes visual images.

believed—how could the mind know what the body was experiencing? How does light hitting the eye become an image in the mind? Descartes' answer was that the animal spirits flow through the brain, and the mind reads the patterns in the flow. When light moves through the lens of the eye, Descartes argued, it affects the way the animal spirits flow through the veins in the back of the eye. When that disturbance in the flow of animal spirits makes it to the brain, the mind sees the unusual pattern and is able to decode it as an image. In the same way, Descartes could explain smell, taste, touch, and hearing.

Animal spirits could not account for free will—humans' ability to determine their own actions—but they did not have to. That was the role of the soul. And, of course, if the soul makes the choices, then it is only proper that the soul be held to account in the ultimate judgment. It all seemed perfect. The pieces fit together so well. Descartes had crafted *The World* just as he wanted it, and he knew the best way

René Descartes

to introduce the work. The first copy would be a Christmas present for his friend Mersenne.

Descartes was putting on the finishing touches and getting ready to send the book when he heard disturbing news from Rome. In June 1633 the Italian astronomer and physicist Galileo Galilei—the most famous scientist of the day—had been condemned by the Inquisition. Officially called the Congregation of the Holy Office, the Inquisition was an institution established by the pope and composed of cardinals and other high-ranking church officials. Its task was to root out heresy.

Galileo ran afoul of the Inquisition with the 1632 publication of his book *Dialogue Concerning the Two Chief Systems of the World*. The book promoted the heliocentric, or sun-centered, model of the universe first proposed by Nicolaus Copernicus. Following the Aristotelian view, church doctrine held that all heavenly bodies move around the earth.

Galileo Galilei

Decades earlier, however, Galileo had concluded that the church's position was wrong. Using an improved telescope of his own design, Galileo discovered three moons

Profiles in Mathematics

orbiting the planet Jupiter—disproving the notion that all heavenly bodies move around the earth. He also observed that, like the moon, the planet Venus has a complete set of phases, which could only be possible if both Venus and the earth were orbiting the sun.

In 1616 the Inquisition had warned Galileo not to promote the Copernican theory. This was a serious matter: the Inquisition could, and sometimes did, mete out serious punishment to those who questioned the earth-centered model of the universe. For espousing Copernicanism the Italian philosopher Tommaso Campanella was imprisoned and tortured; his countryman Giordano Bruno was burned at the stake.

By renouncing his "errors," Galileo escaped a similar fate in 1633, after Inquisition officials found him guilty of heretical views. He remained under house arrest until his death, and his *Dialogue Concerning the Two Chief Systems of the World* was placed on the church's Index of Banned Books. This meant that even reading the book would be considered heresy.

Descartes was stunned to learn of the outcome of Galileo's trial. "I have quasi resolved to burn all my papers or at least not to show them to anyone," he wrote to Mersenne. "I cannot imagine that [Galileo] . . . could have been labeled a criminal for nothing other than wanting to establish the movement of the earth."

Descartes decided that, under the circumstances, he could not go ahead with the publication of *The World*, which included the Copernican view that the earth moves around the sun. Though he had no wish to be branded a heretic, this decision was not taken primarily out of fear for his personal safety—in Protestant Holland, Descartes was beyond the

René Descartes

reach of the Roman Inquisition. Rather, he could see no way to reconcile his work with church doctrine, and he remained a faithful Catholic. "I confess that if [the Copernican view] is false," he wrote to Mersenne, "then all the principles of my philosophy are false also. . . . And because I would not want for anything in the world to be the author of a work where there was the slightest word of which the Church might disapprove, I would rather suppress it altogether than have it appear incomplete—'crippled,' as it were."

Descartes' four-year effort to create a philosophical system that would explain the workings of the entire world with absolute certainty had come to a less-than-satisfactory end. Yet he remained convinced of the value of his work. He would continue his quest for certainty. And, just as he had done following his Saint Martin's Eve dreams in 1619, he would begin anew, rebuilding his thought from its very foundations.

six

The Big Breakthrough

In the aftermath of Galileo's trial, Descartes thought back to an earlier time in his intellectual journey. Following his momentous dreams of November 10, 1619, he had given himself two challenges: first, come up with a new method of reasoning that could be applied to all questions to yield certain knowledge; and second, apply that new method and begin to derive the knowledge. In the quiet warmth of the stove-heated room in Bohemia, he had realized that this would require tearing down the old structure of thought to erect a new one.

Now Descartes realized that he had to do with his own work what he had earlier set out to do with the entire history of thought. He had to tear it all down and start again at the very beginning. But he needed first to figure out what it was he was looking for.

René Descartes

This, at least, he knew: he was looking for absolute certainty. So his question became, What can I know that cannot be doubted? Over the next several years, still moving from residence to residence in Holland, he worked assiduously and finally came up with what he thought was the solution. In doing so, he completely revolutionized philosophy and mathematics. He not only came up with new mathematical tools and a philosophical justification for them, but also showed how these tools could completely change the uses of mathematics. Suddenly, questions in physics could be solved mathematically, not philosophically. The way people looked at the world would be changed forever as a result. Descartes' groundbreaking ideas from this period constitute his greatest contributions to the history of thought and place him among the greatest thinkers in human history.

During this period Descartes, as was his custom, conducted his work alone. He also remained something of a recluse in his private life. However, in late 1634, at the age of thirty-eight, he had a relationship with a young maid employed by the family in Amsterdam with whom he was staying. Descartes never married, and some scholars believe that this was the only romantic attachment of his adult life. In any event, the maid, Helena Jans, gave birth to a daughter in July of 1635. The girl was named Francine. Descartes never publicly acknowledged that he was Francine's father—he pretended she was his niece—but he does appear to have spent some time with the girl. And according to an early biographer, Descartes planned to send her to France to be educated. Sadly, she died of scarlet fever in 1640. Descartes would later serve as an official witness at the wedding of Helena Jans.

Profiles in Mathematics

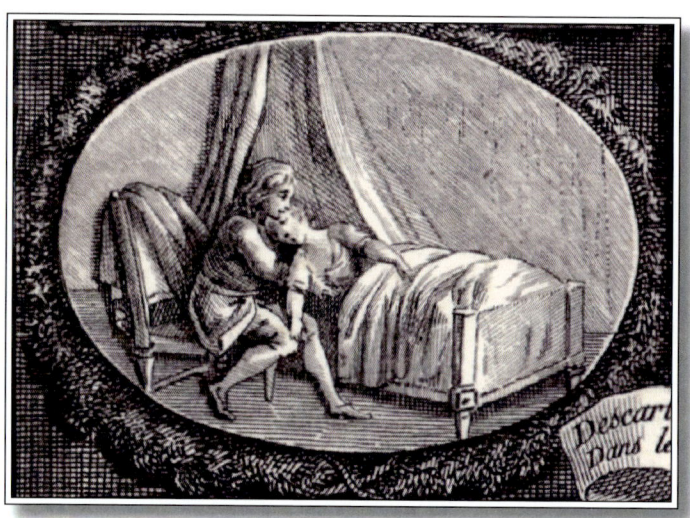

A depiction of Descartes by the bedside of his dying daughter, Francine *(Courtesy of World History Archive/Alamy)*

Three years before his daughter's death, in 1637, Descartes' first published book appeared. *Discourse on the Method for Conducting One's Reason Well and for Seeking Truth in the Sciences* included essays on optics, geometry, and meteorology. Descartes had intended the first section, the *Discourse on Method*, as a preface to the scientific pieces. But it would become famous in its own right. The *Discourse on Method* outlined Descartes' ideas about establishing a philosophical system on the most solid foundation possible, which he expanded in *Meditations on First Philosophy* (1641).

Descartes began his description of the general method by which he guided his reason with a simple statement of what was ultimately desired: absolute certainty. Nothing less would do.

His first guiding principle, Descartes wrote, "was never to accept anything as true that I did not plainly know to be such; that is to say, carefully avoid hasty judgment and prejudice; and to include nothing more in my judgments than what

René Descartes

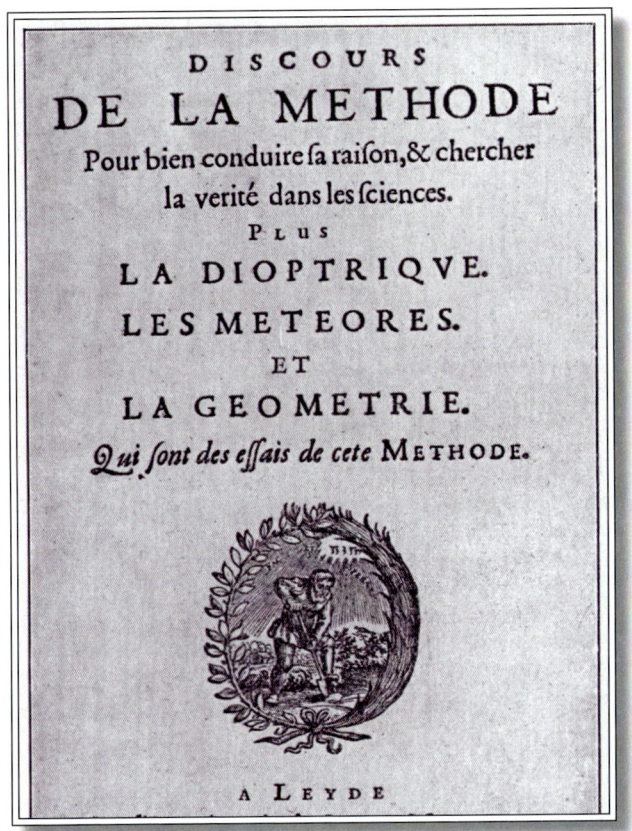

The frontispiece of the original version of Descartes' *Discourse on the Method for Conducting One's Reason Well and for Seeking Truth in the Sciences*

presented itself to my mind so clearly and so distinctly that I had no occasion to call it in doubt." Descartes would, for the sake of this project, think of anything that might possibly be false as if it were false. He wanted to determine what he could know that was absolutely and necessarily true. So if it was possible to have even the most absurd, remote doubt about a proposition or belief, it would be rejected. Was there anything, Descartes wondered, that he could believe without there being any chance that he might be mistaken?

Profiles in Mathematics

Descartes considered the beliefs he held that were based on observation or perception. Could these possibly be wrong? He concluded that there were two grounds to suppose they could. First, observation relies on the senses, and the senses can be fooled—consider optical illusions, for example. Second, the thoughts and objects experienced in a dream often seem indistinguishable from those experienced while awake. "How often does my evening slumber persuade me of such ordinary things as these: that I am here, clothed in my dressing gown, seated next to the fireplace—when in fact I am lying undressed in bed!" Descartes noted. Dreams sometimes simulate reality so perfectly, in fact, that a sleeping person believes he or she is awake. Thus any given perception, regardless of its vividness, might be an illusion.

Descartes was not suggesting that people could be dreaming all the time, or that the senses mislead all (or even most) of the time. But because his method required him to reject any belief about which he could not be 100 percent certain, he was forced to eliminate all knowledge gathered through observation and perception. That was quite a bit. In essence, the existence of everything in the material world—friends, houses, stars, even his own body—had to be treated as false because it was experienced via potentially unreliable sensations.

Without the entire material world, was everything lost? Could anything be known with certainty?

Descartes considered the case of beliefs arising not from the senses but from the mind itself. Truths about logic and mathematics, for example, might be reached by reasoning alone. "For whether I am awake or asleep," he observed, "two plus three make five and a square does not have more than four sides." Geometry is all about lines and circles. And while pictures and diagrams may be useful for references, the real mathematical work is done through abstract reasoning about abstract things.

Line segments, for example, are sets of points that are perfectly straight, and while a line segment has length, it does not have width. Lines on a chalkboard or a piece of paper are not real lines, just representations of them, as every printed or drawn "line" has a finite width and is not exactly straight.

Yet geometers know many facts about the properties of these perfect geometric objects that have never been seen. The same holds true for numbers. It is possible to know that 1 million plus 1 million is 2 million without having counted out 1 million things, another 1 million things, put the two piles together, and counted 2 million things. Both geometric and arithmetic truths do not require observation, just pure thought. Since they do not require the use of flawed human senses, maybe beliefs like this could meet Descartes' requirements for absolute certainty.

Again, however, Descartes found cause to doubt beliefs from reason alone. People make mistakes in reasoning, he observed, even with basic problems in geometry. There was no basis to suppose that any person would be totally immune from such errors.

In *Meditations*, published in 1641, Descartes offered a much more hypothetical—and stranger—argument for doubting that anything based on reasoning could be known with complete certainty. Suppose, he said, there exists an evil demon capable of controlling people's thoughts and bent on deception. "I will suppose therefore that not God,

Profiles in Mathematics

who is supremely good and the source of truth, but rather some malicious demon of the utmost power and cunning has employed all his energies in order to deceive me," Descartes wrote. "I shall think that the sky, the air, the earth, colours, shapes, sounds, and all external things are merely the delusions of dreams which he has devised in order to ensnare my judgement." Perhaps three plus two actually equals six, but the evil demon makes people certain that it equals five. Again, Descartes was not suggesting that the existence of a malicious, all-powerful demon was likely. But that possibility could not be absolutely disproved. Therefore, some doubt would always be attached to every belief.

In his quest for certainty, Descartes had torn down the philosophical basis of all knowledge, and it was unclear whether anything remained upon which he could build. "I suppose, accordingly," he wrote, "that all the things which I see are false (fictitious); I believe that none of those objects which my fallacious memory represents ever existed; I suppose that I possess no senses; I believe that body, figure, extension, motion, and place are merely fictions of my mind. What is there, then, that can be esteemed true? Perhaps this only, that there is absolutely nothing certain."

But Descartes realized that there was *one* thing that he could be completely certain of, one proposition that could not possibly be false: he existed. If he tried to doubt this proposition, then he could ask, *Who* is doubting that I exist? Doubting is a form of thinking, and thinking cannot occur without a subject doing the thinking—in other words, without a thinker. As Descartes famously wrote, "I think, therefore I am."

But what was the "I" of which Descartes spoke? It was

René Descartes

not the self as traditionally conceived, for an evil demon could be deceiving Descartes about everything, including the belief that he had a body. All Descartes had demonstrated beyond doubt was the existence of his own mind. This did not seem a sufficient foundation on which to rebuild all human knowledge.

However, Descartes next considered what it was he thought about. One of those things, he noted, was God. In thinking about God, Descartes envisaged a perfect being. Such a being would be all-knowing (and would know that he knew everything), so he would never have occasion for doubt. Doubt is a sign of imperfection.

Descartes knew that he was capable of doubt and was, therefore, not perfect. Yet he had the idea of a perfect being. Descartes reasoned that this idea could not have come from him because it was more perfect than he was. The only possible source would be something as perfect as the idea. Hence, there must also exist something other than him, something absolutely perfect. The absolutely perfect being is what people call God, and so, Descartes concluded, God must exist.

Additionally, since lying is a bad thing and God is perfect, God cannot be a deceiver. The thoughts Descartes had in his mind did not all come from Descartes himself. He could dream up some things, but those things could be changed at will. He could, for instance, imagine a purple unicorn and then just as easily change it to a white unicorn. But this was not true with other things, such as a horse standing in front of him. These things must have an external source. God must be the ultimate source of what is outside, and, since God is not a deceiver, he would never allow someone to be fooled by an evil demon. Therefore, Descartes concluded,

Profiles in Mathematics

all clear and distinct beliefs are trustworthy. Individual facts from reason and observation can be trusted because of the perfection of God. Any reasoning done based on them is open to error because humans are imperfect and fallible, but the very basics of logic and the simplest observations must be true.

Hence, Descartes could proceed logically from basic first principles—whose truth, he had demonstrated, was underwritten by the perfection of God—and arrive at certainty in all fields of study. Descartes now needed to find those basic first truths that are clear and distinct and from them use pure logic to derive all other truths. This method is what Descartes gave to the world, and it is what he tried to apply to all fields of study.

He reduced groups of complex beliefs to a very small number of basic and indisputable beliefs. From those, all other truths could be logically derived. This idea of reduction was the key.

It was an idea Descartes had used before when solving the problem of mean proportionals. In that case, he had translated the problem from geometry to algebra. In other words, he had reduced a question about lines and lengths into a problem about equations and numbers. This allowed him to give an exact, certain result.

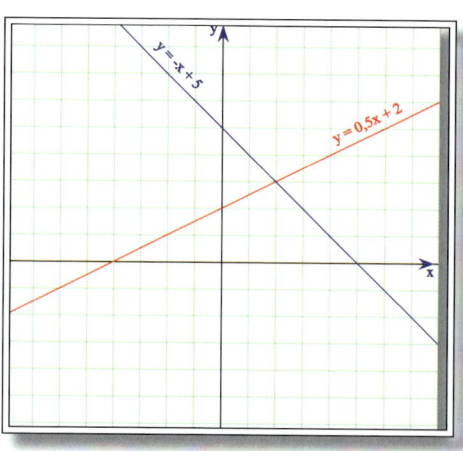

A graph of an equation

René Descartes

Descartes set about applying the technique he had used to solve the problem of mean proportionals to all of geometry. He figured out a general method to translate any problem in geometry into a question of algebra. The idea of "graphing an equation" comes from Descartes' groundbreaking work. Today it all seems obvious: take two perpendicular lines, and call one the x-axis and the other the y-axis. Give every point on the xy-plane an address that is an ordered pair of numbers (x, y) based on how far over and how far up or down it is from the point where the axes intersect, the origin. In certain cases, a set of ordered pairs can be specified by an equation. For example, for any straight line on the xy-plane, all points will have the same ratio of x value to y value. For any of those points, the y value will equal $mx+b$, where m is the slope of the line (how much it rises on the y-axis for every one unit it runs along the x-axis) and b is the value of the y coordinate at the point where the line hits the y-axis. That this was possible and useful, though, was far from obvious, and it took a mathematical mind of Descartes' magnitude to first figure it out.

As a result of Descartes' work, every geometric shape could be represented by a set of points. Truths about geometric objects could be turned into equations. Whereas the old Euclidean geometry could deal only with questions about the relations of regular and simple shapes, now there was a way to answer questions about complex, even arbitrary shapes. The method of translation, analytic geometry, was incredibly powerful.

Geometry could apply to physical systems. A cannonball, for example, does not move in a straight line but along a curve because of the pull of gravity. This path, or trajectory, could be converted into an equation. As a result, questions about

Profiles in Mathematics

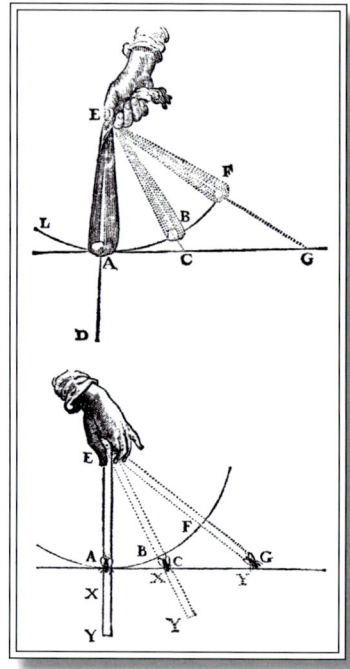

This diagram from one of Descartes' works illustrates the trajectory of a moving object.

how high and far the cannonball would travel, and how long it would stay in the air, could be answered. The ability to translate the complex paths of actual objects made robust mathematical physics a possibility for the first time in history. Instead of looking like philosophy, science would now look like mathematics and yield exact solutions with exact predictions.

The power of Descartes' new system, created for purely philosophical reasons, was stretching the human imagination. He had finally found, for a large swath of the intellectual landscape, the certainty he had sought his entire life. As he applied his method to questions of physics, Descartes began obtaining precise results. Unfortunately, his success would generate controversy and a string of bitter disputes with other scholars.

seven
Friends and Enemies

When Descartes had lived in Paris, one of the intellectuals there who most impressed him was the writer Jean-Louis Guez de Balzac. The two had become friends, and they exchanged many letters over the years. Descartes admired—and strove to imitate—Balzac's ability to convey deep, philosophically rich ideas in simple language. Descartes disliked writers who made their work unnecessarily complex. Thus, when he wrote the *Discourse on Method*, Descartes did everything he could to make it accessible not just to university trained scholars but also to average readers. Descartes published the book in French rather than in the academic language of Latin because, as he explained, "I hope that those who use only their natural reason in all its purity will judge my opinions better than those who believe only in old books."

In France, however, the *Discourse on Method* was read widely by scholars—and most did not judge the work

Profiles in Mathematics

Jean-Louis Guez de Balzac
(Courtesy of Roger Viollet/Getty Images)

positively, especially the work in mathematics. Leading the charge against Descartes was Pierre de Fermat, who would become a famous mathematician in his own right. Fermat, who was also friendly with Mersenne, would use their shared acquaintance to convey his sharply worded objections, and Fermat always had plenty of objections when it came to Descartes' work.

Around Fermat was a circle of friends who likewise disapproved of Descartes' writings. They argued that most of what Descartes presented was either obscure or wrong. What was correct in it, they claimed, Descartes had plagiarized from the mathematician François Viète. Descartes argued that while he had read Viète's work, his was so far superior in being more general and powerful that the suggestion of stealing was completely absurd. Descartes showed little patience for his detractors and treated them quite harshly in his correspondence. Of one detractor Descartes said, "One should

René Descartes

Pierre de Fermat *(Courtesy of Mary Evans Picture Library/Alamy)*

allow little dogs to bark without bothering to resist them." Of another he wrote, "I have never seen anything from him which could not serve to prove his incompetence."

If Descartes was scorned in France, he won supporters in Holland. Among those who championed Descartes' new

Profiles in Mathematics

François Viète

philosophical method was Henri Reneri, a professor of philosophy at Utrecht University. The two became lifelong friends, and for a period Descartes took up residence in Utrecht to be able to visit and converse with Reneri.

Reneri became the first university professor to teach Descartes' works. It was from Reneri's lectures that Descartes would gain one of his most devoted followers, Henri Regius. A professor of medicine, Regius was intrigued by what he heard of the French scholar from Reneri. He read all of Descartes' published writings and tried to apply the lessons to his own studies and in his own teaching. Regius began to achieve great academic success. The number of students attending his lectures grew significantly, and he received the prestigious position of "Extraordinary Chair of Theoretical Medicine" at Utrecht University.

Regius was so thrilled by this appointment that he wrote an extremely flattering letter to Descartes, in which he asked whether he might meet the man to whom he attributed his success. Descartes agreed. He was clearly pleased that in Holland, at least, his work was being appreciated.

The zeal with which Regius promoted the Cartesian approach, however, led to difficulties. Even in Protestant Holland, the classical world view was deeply entrenched in the universities, and Descartes' work challenged that world view. Regius's teaching angered influential academics. Among them was Gisbertus Voetius, the senior professor of theology at Utrecht and one of the university's most powerful voices. Staunchly Protestant and a deeply nationalistic Dutchman, Voetius was not predisposed to approve of a Catholic foreigner like Descartes. After Regius arranged a series of public debates about Descartes' writings on biology and human physiology—and took it upon himself to defend the Cartesian approach—Voetius declared Descartes' ideas dangerous. They led to atheism, he asserted.

Profiles in Mathematics

The situation turned worse for Descartes in 1641, when Voetius was made rector of Utrecht University. Voetius convinced the academic senate of the university to pass an official condemnation of Descartes' work, thereby prohibiting it from being taught in any class.

But Voetius did not stop there. He spread vicious rumors about Descartes, who became a hated man. Descartes was referred to as the French liar, and Regius as the French liar's monkey. Descartes was growing exasperated: the Dutch objected because his work was too Catholic; the Catholics objected because he supported Copernicus, making his work not Catholic enough; and other French mathematicians objected seemingly for the sake of objecting.

When Voetius accused him of plagiarism, Descartes had finally had enough. It was time to fight back. Descartes publicly declared Voetius a vicious liar and slanderer. Voetius responded by bringing official charges of slander against Descartes.

The town council of Utrecht was clearly slanted in favor of one of the most powerful and respected members of the community—especially when his complaint was against a foreigner, and a Catholic one at that. The council arranged to put Descartes on trial. Descartes argued that because he did not reside in Utrecht, Utrecht's town council had no jurisdiction over the matter. The council passed judgment anyway, finding Descartes guilty. The punishment would be expulsion from the country and the burning of his books.

Angry at this turn of events, Descartes decided to pull some strings. He traveled to The Hague, the capital of Holland, where he knew he had an old friend in a very high place. Descartes spoke with Prince Maurice, his for-

René Descartes

Utrecht, Netherlands, circa 1900 *(Library of Congress)*

mer military commander. When the magistrates of Utrecht received a personal letter from the Prince of Orange, the town council found itself in an extremely difficult position. On one side was the most powerful person in the town; on the other, one of the most powerful in the nation. The council decided to reopen the case and leave it undecided. Descartes was found neither innocent nor guilty.

Prince Maurice's intervention had helped Descartes resolve his legal difficulties. The interest of one of the prince's relatives would help Descartes refine his philosophy.

Descartes once described his approach to writing by saying that he wanted to make his words so clear that even a

Profiles in Mathematics

woman could understand them. Little did he realize that a woman would understand his work better than anyone else. Princess Elizabeth of Bohemia was fluent in French and had read Descartes' books with a favorable eye. When she heard that Regius would be lecturing at the university in The Hague, she summoned him and quizzed him about Descartes' work. Regius was stumped by a philosophical question and suggested that she ask Descartes himself.

Elizabeth, in her mid-twenties at the time of her meeting with Regius, was a formidable figure. A perceptive thinker, she had from an early age devoted herself to her studies, learning French, English, Dutch, Latin, and Greek. Later she received private lessons in philosophy and the sciences from professors at the university in The Hague. Elizabeth also had an impressive lineage. Her great-grandmother was Mary, Queen of Scots; her grandfather, James I of England. Frederick V, her father, had been the Protestant king of Bohemia until he was overthrown by Catholic forces—the same forces Descartes was serving with when he had his life-changing dreams in 1619. After his defeat at White Mountain, Frederick and his family, including Elizabeth, were forced into exile in Holland. There the princess and her siblings ended up under the protection of Prince Maurice, their uncle.

In May 1643 Elizabeth wrote a letter to Descartes in which she raised the question Regius had been unable to answer. The question concerned a fundamental problem with Descartes' world view—what has come to be called the problem of interaction. Descartes argued that each human being is a combination of 1) a material body that functions like a machine in perfect accordance with the laws of physics; and 2) an immaterial soul—or, to use a term with fewer

René Descartes

religious connotations, a mind—that is not a physical entity and therefore is not subject to the laws of physics. Yet the mind could command motion in the muscles—and thereby enable humans to move, speak, eat, and perform other physical actions according to the mind's will. It did this by affecting the flow of animal spirits, the substance that Descartes believed conveys bodily sensations to the mind and animates the nerves. Descartes speculated that the pineal gland, deep in the brain, was the point where the body and mind interacted via the animal spirits.

Yet in his writings on physics, Descartes stated that motion is imparted to material objects through collisions with other material objects. In her letter, Princess Elizabeth asked a very perceptive question: If the mind has no size, shape, or weight as it is immaterial, how could it collide with and cause the motion of animal spirits, which are material?

Descartes responded to the princess with a highly complimentary letter.

> The honour your Highness does me in sending her commandments in writing is greater than I ever dared hope; and it is more consoling to my unworthiness than the other favour which I had hoped for passionately, which was to receive them by word of mouth. If I had been permitted to pay homage to you and offer you my very humble services when I was last at the Hague, I would have had too many wonders to admire at the same time.

After the flattery, he attempted to answer her question with an analogy. Most interactions between objects are indeed the result of collisions, he said. But just as gravitation causes a body to move without something touching it, so too could

Profiles in Mathematics

the mind affect and be affected by the animal spirits without physical contact between the two. Descartes ended the letter with an offer to travel to The Hague to speak personally to the princess, if she so desired. And of course, she did.

The two became quite friendly. Descartes was living in the country not far from The Hague, making the journey short enough for day trips. More frequently, however, the princess traveled to Descartes' residence for their meetings. Soon the reclusive Descartes moved farther from The Hague, effectively ending Elizabeth's visits.

Nevertheless, he and the princess continued to exchange very detailed and philosophically challenging letters. Back and forth they debated, Elizabeth always adopting the tone of an unschooled amateur while asking extremely sophisticated questions. Discussing religion, philosophy, and science by mail, Descartes became her friend, her teacher, and her intellectual sparring partner.

Descartes even gave Elizabeth—who suffered from a number of illnesses—medical advice based on his theories about human physiology. She gratefully reported that his advice from afar had been more effective than the prescriptions of her doctors. What Elizabeth gave to Descartes was quite different: the conviction to tackle a topic he had long avoided.

eight
The Certainties of Space and Death

Descartes was never one to shy away from intellectual controversy. He waged protracted and bitter verbal battles with critics of his work—and never conceded defeat. But after the trial of Galileo, there was one topic even he dared not touch: astronomy.

He was caught in a bind. The Catholic Church had made perfectly clear that an earth-centered model of the universe was to be accepted as true by all the faithful and that dissent would not be tolerated. Furthermore, Descartes, unlike Galileo, in no way sought to oppose papal authority on the matter. But at the same time, the evidence was pointing ever more clearly toward Copernicus's sun-centered picture. What Descartes wanted more than anything else was a synthesis of science and his religion. He believed that the two were not competitors for truth, as most people considered them to be, but complementary. Theology provided truths of the

Profiles in Mathematics

immaterial realm, and science provided truths of the physical world. The trick was to figure out how they fit together.

Although his intentions were nothing short of pious, Descartes knew that if he dared to approach the thorny issue of astronomy, he had better be clever, he had better be respectful and reverent, and, most of all, he had better be right. The method behind his system was intentionally designed to produce unquestionable certainty, and if his views deviated at all from strict orthodoxy, the supporting arguments behind them needed to be ironclad. With this in mind, he published a book in 1644 titled *The Principles of Philosophy*, in which he worked out his views on space, gravity, and the universe.

Descartes viewed space as the distance between two objects. The defining characteristic of space is extension—length, breadth, and height. To measure the distance between two points or the volume of some region is to measure the amount of space. Thus for Descartes, space becomes not just the place where things are, but an entity in itself.

In this view, it is logically impossible to conceive of a vacuum. No matter what region is examined, space is present, even if nothing else is there. Empty space is not really empty; it is full of space. Descartes therefore considered the universe to be a plenum—that is, a completely filled volume. "That a vacuum in the philosophical sense of the term (that is, a space in which there is absolutely no [material] substance) cannot exist is evident from the fact that the extension of space, or of internal place, does not differ from the extension of body," Descartes maintained. "From the sole fact that a body is extended in length, breadth, and depth; we rightly conclude that it is a substance: because it is entirely

René Descartes

contradictory for that which is nothing to possess extension. And the same must be concluded about space which is said to be empty: that, since it certainly has extension, there must necessarily also be substance in it."

Within this space, Descartes said, all objects move only when pushed. This was in direct contradiction to Aristotle's account of mechanics. Aristotle said the source of motion was internal. All objects, the Greek philosopher believed, were made up of one of five elements, and those elements had natural places. Earth and water, the heavy elements, had their natural place at the center of the earth, the center of the universe. Fire and air, the light elements, had their natural places around the earth, just inside of the sphere that

Descartes' universe *(Courtesy of The Print Collector/Alamy)*

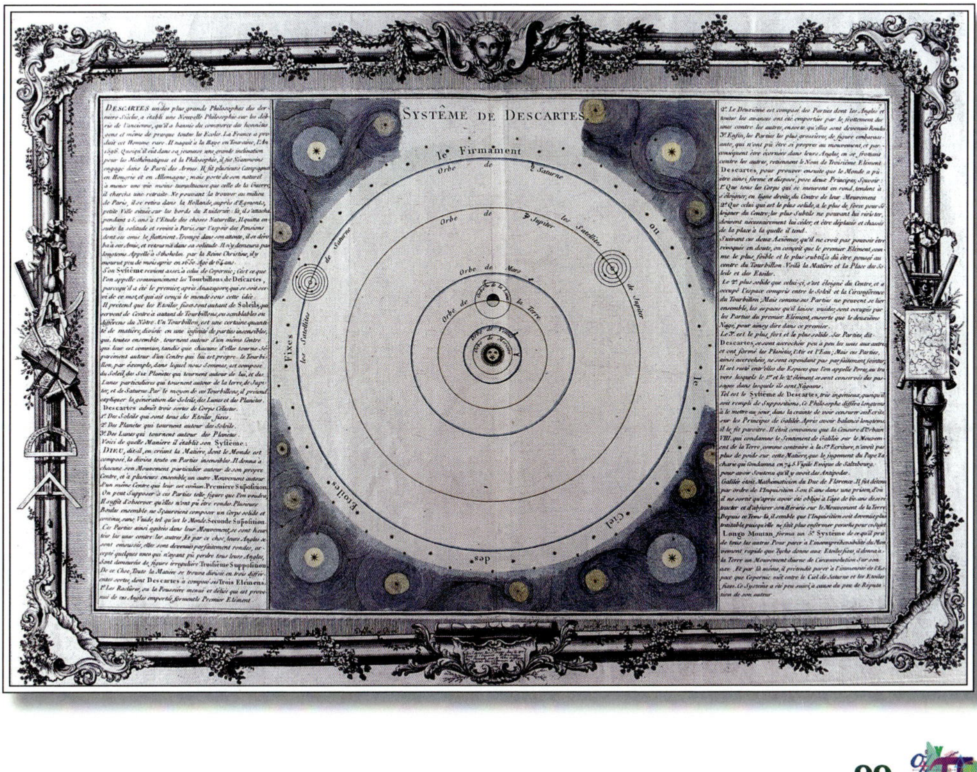

Profiles in Mathematics

defines the orbit of the moon. When removed from their natural place, objects will move in straight lines (the shortest possible path) in the direction of their natural place. Water spilled from a cup moves straight down because there is an internal desire on the part of the water to find its way to the center of the earth, where it belongs. Similarly, the flame on a torch will point upward no matter whether the torch is held straight up, sideways, or upside down, because the fire is seeking its natural place away from the center of the earth. In Aristotle's conception, all heavenly bodies—the moon, the sun, the stars, and the planets—are made of a more perfect element called aether. Aether's natural motion is circles, because circles are more perfect than straight lines. This is why the sun, moon, and stars rise and set, Aristotle believed. The motion in all of these cases comes from inside the object moving, not from some outside force. When there was an external force, it would move a body, but the instant the external force was removed, the body would resume its natural motion in a circle or straight line to its natural place.

Descartes rejected this view and argued that there is no such thing as a natural place for any sort of object. An object at rest—regardless of whether it is a star or a drop of water—will not move if it does not experience any force upon it. But once there is a force pushing or pulling it, the object will move. "[E]ach thing, as far as is in its power, always remains in the same state; and that consequently, when it is once moved, it always continues to move," Descartes wrote. The greater the force, the faster the object moves. When the force is removed, the object will continue to move in the same state of motion until some other force changes its motion.

René Descartes

Descartes said that the source of movement comes not from within the body itself, as Aristotle thought, but rather from the effect of other bodies on it.

In this way, Descartes could answer a problem that had plagued Aristotle's theory for centuries: the arrow. When an arrow is set in a bow and the archer pulls it back and lets it go, the tension in the bowstring pushes the arrow. This causes it to move forward. But the instant it leaves the bow, the string no longer acts on the arrow. According to Aristotle's theory, the arrow should immediately fall straight to the ground, seeking its natural place. Aristotle tried to explain why this did not happen. Air displaced by the advancing tip of the arrow, he said, moves around and pushes the arrow from behind. But this account was hard to swallow. Descartes, on the other hand, explained that the string conveys motion to the arrow. The arrow maintains this motion as it leaves the bow and flies. Such an account was much more likely to be true.

This mechanical picture fit in perfectly with Descartes' earlier views. But there was one problem—the arrow does not continue in a straight line. Instead, it gently arcs toward the ground. It is affected by gravity. Gravity presented a problem for Descartes because there does not seem to be anything doing the pushing. If all motion is the result of forces from contact, what is a falling object in contact with?

Part of the answer is the surrounding air. During Descartes' time, experiments were being done showing how air pressure varies at different altitudes and can be affected by temperature. Descartes was aware of this work, having met with some of the famous experimenters on his travels through Europe. But there was a problem with using air pressure as

Profiles in Mathematics

his explanation. He knew that air pressure is less at higher altitudes, but the gravitational force on objects did not seem to lessen accordingly. Air pressing against objects could not be what caused them to fall.

Additionally, Descartes believed the force pulling water toward the earth must be the same force that moved the sun, moon, and stars. In space there would not be air to do this. But if air could not be the source of the motion, then what was doing the pushing? Descartes concluded that it must be space itself. Massive bodies must have an effect on space, causing currents in it. The pressure from these currents of space, he believed, were what moved objects in straight lines close to the earth and in circular paths away from the earth. The effect would be much like what happens when a drain is opened in a sink full of water. Close to the drain, objects are sucked by the rushing water straight in toward the center of the drain. Farther away, however, the water spirals, causing vortices. An object caught up in such a vortex would revolve around the center of the drain in a circular orbit, dragged along by the water.

If space acts like water in a sink, that would explain both the straight-line motion of objects near the earth and the circular orbits of bodies in space. And if all large bodies generated these vortices in space, then it would not only be the earth that objects would revolve around. Jupiter's vortex explained the movement of its moons. The earth's vortex captured the moon, and the sun had a vortex that dragged around the earth and the other planets.

But there was a big problem. Descartes' explanation had the earth moving around the sun. Putting that idea forward had gotten Galileo into a great deal of trouble with the Catholic

René Descartes

Church. However, when Descartes closely read the details of the judgment against Galileo, he noticed that the Italian was convicted of heresy not for saying that the earth orbited the sun, but for saying that the earth moved. What Descartes needed was a way to explain how the earth could go around the sun without moving. This was impossible—unless the concept of motion was understood in a different way.

As he thought about the problem, Descartes recognized that motion involves a change of place. If a person goes from one location to another, the person has moved. "[A] man, seated in a ship which is sailing out of port, thinks that he is moving if he turns his attention to the shores, which he considers to be at rest," Descartes observed. At the same time, however, the man on the ship does not think he is moving "if he turns his attention to the parts of the ship, in relation to which he constantly maintains the same situation." So motion is defined relative to something else that is defined as stationary. There is no real motion, only motion relative to something else.

What Descartes needed for his description of planetary motion was something that would determine real location. It could not be an object, since all objects themselves could be moved. But if not an object, then what? Descartes decided that it had to be space itself. Motion, he said, is a change in location relative to space. To go from one point of space to another point of space is to change location, and thus to move. It would seem, then, that in revolving around the sun, the earth moves.

For Descartes, however, space itself is an entity and is affected by objects with mass. Space, Descartes believed, forms vortices around large objects. The earth is caught in

103

the sun's vortex and is dragged around, so in one sense it does move. But the earth itself has a vortex, and this vortex keeps hold of the very same bit of space. Since motion is a change in location relative to space itself, and since the space around the earth remains the same, the earth can orbit the sun without ever moving. Descartes could say that the pope had it exactly right: the earth does not move. At the same time, Descartes could hold a Copernican view, saying the earth orbits the sun. He had reconciled science with the official teachings of the Catholic Church.

At least, he thought he had. But Descartes was still nervous about how his work would be received. Once *Principles of Philosophy* was published, he sent copies of the book, along with personal notes, to Jesuit professors he thought would be sympathetic to his work. Among them was his old friend Father Charlet. In these letters, Descartes tried to explain that while his views might seem shocking at first, they were actually in the tradition of Aristotle and, he claimed, did not violate any Aristotelian principles.

Nevertheless, *Principles of Philosophy* did not receive the warm welcome Descartes had hoped for. Rather, it ignited a new wave of criticism.

Descartes' position was not helped by the fact that his disciple Regius was about to publish a book of his own. In his book, Regius acknowledged his great debt to Descartes and portrayed himself as working along the same lines. His views, however, were much more unorthodox than those of his hero, especially his claim that the human soul died with the body. These sorts of assertions were sure to cause the kind of trouble that Descartes wanted to avoid. The memory of the episode in Holland was still fresh, and Descartes did not wish for a repeat performance. He had to distance himself from Regius as much as possible.

Descartes was once again in the familiar, uncomfortable position of having his views criticized by the authorities in both France and Holland. He seemed trapped. But then he discovered that another powerful figure was interested in his writings: Queen Christina of Sweden.

Keenly intelligent herself, Christina sought to attract the finest minds of Europe to her court. Among these was Descartes. Through mutual friends, including Princess Elizabeth, Christina met Descartes several times, and the two began to correspond.

After discovering Descartes' *Principles of Philosophy* and working through the first sections, Christina decided that she wanted to study the entire work and that such study would be greatly facilitated by the presence of Descartes himself. He was invited to Sweden to become the personal tutor of the queen.

Descartes found the offer attractive. It was made more so by Descartes' continuing troubles in France and Holland. The opportunity to escape to the protective umbrella of a friendly queen was too much to pass up. In 1649 René Descartes traveled to Sweden.

Christina's routine was the opposite of Descartes'. Whereas Descartes had maintained his habit of sleeping well into the morning and filling his days with quiet contemplation, Christina rose early. Her schedule was filled with court business, and she decided that the only time she could fit in her lessons and discussions with Descartes was at 5 A.M. Descartes would have to rise, dress, and walk in the frigid early-morning darkness to the castle.

Descartes (second from right) teaching Queen Christina of Sweden *(Courtesy of Visual Arts Library (London)/Alamy)*

René Descartes

A 1647 portrait of Descartes

The cold environment and disrupted schedule were stresses that may have renewed the lung problems Descartes had experienced as a youngster. Within months of moving to Sweden, he contracted a serious illness that moved to his lungs. He began to suffer greatly, developing a fever and experiencing periods of delirium.

Descartes spent his life searching for certainty, and there is nothing more certain than death. On February 11, 1650, at age fifty-three, René Descartes died of pneumonia.

nine
Shoulders of a Giant

Descartes' death may have brought about an end to his writing, but by no means did it bring about an end to his influence. The intellectual world that Descartes left was transformed because of his work. Philosophy, mathematics, and science proceeded in completely new directions because of the trails that Descartes blazed.

He is most remembered as the "father of modern philosophy" because his influence changed both how philosophy was done and what questions philosophers asked. Before Descartes, philosophy was controlled by professors in church-sponsored universities. The questions they asked were largely metaphysical questions—questions about the nature of reality, primarily about the nature of God and the relation of things in the world to God. The approach of pre-Cartesian philosophers was to look to ancient texts, particularly the ancient Greek philosophers, take their pre-Christian pagan systems

René Descartes

of thought, and attempt to work them into a new structure that would complement church-dictated orthodoxy.

But Descartes changed all of that. Philosophy in the century following Descartes no longer took metaphysical questions as the first ones to be answered. Rather, like Descartes, the thinkers who followed believed that questions about the possibility of knowledge (what philosophers call epistemological questions) must sit at the foundation of philosophy. Before saying what exists, people must determine what kinds of things can be known. And from the basis of that knowledge and nothing more, philosophers began to talk about what they could learn of the reality underneath the observations.

The evil demon problem that Descartes outlined—knowing whether the thoughts in his head accurately depicted the world outside—became one of the central issues for all philosophers. People do not have direct access to the world; all knowledge comes into the mind through the senses. How can a person be sure that what is in her mind resembles the thing that put it there? When a person sees a chair, she has the idea of a chair, but can she know whether the real chair itself actually resembles the image in her thoughts?

Descartes tried to answer this question by proving the existence of a nondeceiving God. Other philosophers found his proof unconvincing and the rest of his argument unsatisfying, but even though they did not accept Descartes' answer, they were convinced that he asked the right question. When Descartes tore down the old structure of thought to rebuild it from the foundations, he was right that the old building should be destroyed. But the project of figuring out what and how to rebuild was beyond the capacity of just one man, even a man

Profiles in Mathematics

as brilliant as Descartes. The resulting discussion dominated philosophical discourse for the following centuries.

In addition to the issues philosophers thought important, Descartes also changed the way they went about thinking. Descartes' focus on method and his invention of a rigorous, logical means to justify philosophical claims set the stage for the development of a stricter, more formal approach to doing philosophy. There are perhaps five figures that not only contributed to philosophy but entirely rerouted its path: in addition to Descartes, only Plato, Aristotle, Immanuel Kant, and Ludwig Wittgenstein influenced the history of thought to the same degree.

One of the reasons that philosophy changed after Descartes was that people's view of the world had changed. Advances in science made the old Aristotelian picture of the world obsolete. The new Copernican image that took humans out of the privileged place at the center of the universe won out. Descartes' view, in which the material world operated according to its own mechanical rules, eliminated the need for theological explanations of natural occurrences.

One world view that remained consistent while still maintaining a belief in God was deism—the belief that God created the universe and left it to run on its own. Like a well-made clock, the universe needed constructing and an initial winding, but after that no divine interaction was required. This view became strongly influential on the thinkers who followed Descartes.

The idea that the world could be understood as a complex, perfectly constructed machine derived support from the successes of Descartes' work in the sciences, especially given the fact that his analytic geometry allowed questions

René Descartes

in the sciences to become mathematically framed. Scientists could now use equations to describe the way natural systems developed. As a result, they could predict new phenomena. By graphing values they measured under different conditions, they could spot regularities they never would have noticed otherwise.

Perhaps two of the greatest scientist-mathematicians of the generation following Descartes were also those who studied

Gottfried Wilhelm von Leibniz *(Courtesy of North Wind Picture Archives/Alamy)*

Profiles in Mathematics

him the closest: Gottfried Wilhelm von Leibniz and Isaac Newton. Both saw the revolutionary quality of Descartes' thought, and both tried to advance it.

Leibniz was a German intellectual who studied with the Dutch physicist-mathematician Christian Huygens. Huygens had met Descartes through Mersenne and had exchanged many letters with him. When Leibniz asked Huygens to train him in mathematics, the Dutchman sent him to read

Sir Isaac Newton

René Descartes

the mathematical and scientific works of Descartes. Indeed, it is from Leibniz's studies and writings that modern scholars know many details about Descartes' lost manuscript for *The World*. Leibniz worked on problems in mathematics, science, and philosophy, but his greatest achievement was the development of what would come to be known as integral calculus.

Integral Calculus

One of the questions that motivated the discovery of integral calculus was how to find the exact area under a curve. With Descartes' analytic geometry, quantities like position and time could be recorded and turned into equations that could be graphed. Questions about the system could then be asked in terms of the graph.

Descartes had argued that motion was conserved. For example, when a bow conveys an amount of motion to an arrow, the motion is maintained in the arrow. Descartes left the idea of "amount of motion" somewhat vague. But the scientists who followed him tried to account for it in terms of the total area under a curve that represented the motion.

From ancient times, it was known that a good approximation of the area under a curve could be obtained by constructing a set of rectangles that almost filled the curve. And figuring out the area of each rectangle was a simple matter of multiplying the length by the height. Adding up all the areas of all the rectangles would yield an approximate

Profiles in Mathematics

answer for the area under the curve. However, because one corner of the rectangle touched the curve and the adjacent corner did not, there would be a small gap between the corner of one rectangle and the next. These gaps represented the deviation of the calculated value from the real value. The thinner the rectangles, the smaller the gaps and the better the approximation.

Leibniz realized that if the rectangles were shrunk until they were infinitesimally thin, the result would be the exact area. The problem is that a rectangle with a width of zero has an area of zero, and so it would take an infinite number of them to fill the region under the curve. Leibniz had to figure out how to add an infinite number of zeros and get a number. The trick was the fundamental theorem of calculus.

If an infinite series of numbers are added together, some yield an infinite sum and others converge on a finite number. For example, the more terms added to the series $1/2 + 1/4 + 1/8 + 1/16 + \ldots + 1/2^n$, the closer and closer the sum gets to the number 1. This series converges to what would later be called a limit, and the limit of this series is 1. Leibniz realized that he could find the series whose limit was the area under the curve.

Isaac Newton first came in contact with Cartesian thought as a student at Cambridge. Although the official curriculum was primarily Aristotelian, Newton, like Descartes, was dissatisfied with classical physics and studied other approaches on his own time. He was fascinated by Descartes' mathematical

René Descartes

approach, which mirrored his own love of Euclid. The idea that there might be mathematical regularities governing the material world was deeply attractive to Newton, even if he had theological objections to Descartes' overall project.

Between 1664 and 1665, Cambridge was closed because of an outbreak of bubonic plague. Newton spent the year living on a farm with his mother. In that time he produced a miraculous body of work: his theory of universal gravitation; his theory of mechanics; his theory of light, which explained the rainbow; and the foundations for what would become differential calculus.

Differential Calculus

One of the problems that led Newton to calculus was the question of how fast an object was moving at any point along its trajectory. It was easy to tell how far something went and how long it took to get there, and those numbers would give an average speed. But for something that accelerated or decelerated during the trip, the question of instantaneous velocity was not something that even Descartes' methods could determine.

Newton realized that for any curve there will be a unique line that touches that curve at only one point—what is called the tangent. If he graphed a curve with time on one axis and distance on the other, then the slope of the tangent (the measure of how steep the angle of the tangent line is) would be an indicator of the projectile's velocity

Profiles in Mathematics

at exactly that point. Any line on this graph would be a measure of distance over time, and a straight line would be constant acceleration. That the line touches the curve at a single point would indicate that at one particular moment those velocities were the same. Additionally, if Newton could figure out how that angle changed along the curve, then he could figure out not only the instantaneous velocity, but also the instantaneous acceleration.

An approximation to this line could be found using a second point nearby the point in question. If he took the difference in position (the difference in height along the vertical axis) and divided it by the difference in time (the difference in length along the horizontal axis), Newton would get an approximation to the quantity he was looking for. The closer together the points, the better the approximation.

Newton realized that he could get what he needed exactly if the distance between the points was made infinitesimally small. But doing this had two effects: the difference in height shrank to zero and so did the difference in length. Newton was dividing zero by zero. Any number with zero in the numerator is zero, and dividing by zero is undefined.

But Newton discovered what Leibniz had also discovered about series of numbers. And with the fundamental theorem of calculus, Newton was able to figure out how to use this method and get exactly what he needed.

Both Newton and Leibniz came to understand how important calculus would be for the future of science, and a battle began over who should receive credit as the father of calculus. The two made the central discoveries independently of each other, and their work went in different directions. In the end Leibniz's name, "calculus," won out over Newton's term ("fluxions"), and Leibniz's notation for the new mathematical system became the standard over Newton's choices. Still, Newton would receive the lion's share of acclaim for the invention of calculus, in part because he used the new branch of mathematics to derive a new theory of physics.

But regardless of who gets the credit for its invention, calculus revolutionized human knowledge. With it, Newton developed a new theory of motion that when paired with his new theory of gravitation was among the most important scientific discoveries in human history. Newton could explain the motion of the planets, the tides, the path of projectiles, and why buildings stood or fell. It was a nearly complete description of the working of the world in terms of mathematical equations.

Newton had done what Descartes had dreamed of. He had mathematized the world, creating the certainty that Descartes had searched for his whole life. When reflecting on this success, Newton said, "If I have seen further it is by standing on [the shoulders] of Giants." Among those giants was René Descartes.

timeline

1596   Born on March 31 in France.

1606   Begins school at La Flèche.

1615   Leaves La Flèche.

1616   Studies law at the University of Poitiers.

1617   First travels to Paris.

1618   Meets Isaac Beeckman on November 10.

1619   On November 10, has three dreams that change his life.

1628   Attends lecture of Chandoux.

1629   Begins writing *Le Monde (The World)*.

1633   Galileo is condemned by the Inquisition; Descartes decides not to publish *Le Monde*.

1637   Descartes publishes *Discourse on Method, Optics, Geometry, and Meteorology*.

1641   Charged with slander by Voetius.

1642   Introduced to Princess Elizabeth.

1644   Publishes *Principles of Philosophy*.

1649   Travels to Sweden at the invitation of Queen Christina.

1650   Dies of pneumonia on February 11.

Sources

CHAPTER ONE: "Nourished on Letters"

p. 16, "I inherited from [my mother] . . ." Desmond Clarke, *Descartes: A Biography* (Cambridge, UK: Cambridge University Press, 2006), 9-10.

p. 17, "good for nothing . . ." Rochford Vrooman, *René Descartes: A Biography* (New York: Putnam, 1970), 23.

p. 17, "When I was a child . . ." Ibid., 26.

p. 18, "acted like a father . . ." Clarke, *Descartes*, 25.

p. 23, "I have been nourished . . ." René Descartes, *Discourse on Method* (Indianapolis: Hackett, 1998), 3.

p. 23, "delighted most of all . . ." Ibid., 4.

p. 23, "did not yet notice . . ." Ibid.

CHAPTER TWO: Reading "The Book of the World"

p. 35, "I completely abandoned . . ." Descartes, *Discourse on Method*, 5–6.

p. 40, "[L]ong chains . . ." Ibid., 11.

p. 41, "Among the sense-objects . . ." René Descartes, *Compendium of Music* (*Compendium Musicae*) (Middleton, WI: American Institute of Musicology, 1961), 13.

CHAPTER THREE: Living a Dream

p. 43, "in a stove-heated room . . ." Descartes, *Discourse on Method*, 7.

119

Profiles in Mathematics

p. 45, "Martin, who is still . . ." Alexander Roberts, trans., "Sulpitius Severus on the Life of St. Martin," http://www.users.csbsju.edu/~eknuth/npnf2-11/sulpitiu/lifeofst.html.

CHAPTER FOUR: Making a Reputation

p. 52, "Plato says one thing. . ." Anthony Kenny, ed., *Philosophical Letters* (Minneapolis: University of Minnesota Press, 1970), 16-17.

p. 58, "You saw these two results . . ." Ibid., 20.

CHAPTER FIVE: Creating *The World*

p. 63, "In this great city . . ." Vrooman, *René Descartes*, 76–77.

p. 68, "You prefer stupid boasting . . ." Clarke, *Descartes*, 49.

p. 68, "I think that the science . . ." Kenny, *Philosophical Letters*, 24.

p. 71, "is turned into spirits . . ." Ibid., 36.

p. 74, "I have quasi resolved . . ." Vrooman, *René Descartes*, 84.

p. 75, "I confess that . . ." Ibid.

CHAPTER SIX: The Big Breakthrough

p. 78, "was never to accept anything . . ." Descartes, *Discourse on Method*, 11.

p. 80, "How often . . ." René Descartes, *Meditations on First Philosophy* (Indianapolis: Hackett, 1998), 60.

p. 80-81, "For whether I am awake . . ." Ibid., 61.

p. 81-82, "I will suppose . . ." René Descartes, *Selected Philosophical Writings*, ed. John Cottingham, Robert Stoothoff, and Dugald Murdoch (Cambridge, UK: Cambridge University Press, 1988), 79.

p. 82, "I suppose, accordingly . . ." Descartes, *Meditations*, 63.

p. 82, "I think, therefore I am," Descartes, *Discourse on Method*, 18.

CHAPTER SEVEN: Friends and Enemies

p. 87, "I hope that those . . ." Descartes, *Discourse on Method*, 43.

p. 88-89, "One should allow little dogs . . ." Clarke, *Descartes*, 173.

p. 89, "I have never seen . . ." Vrooman, *René Descartes*, 121.

p. 95, "The honour your Highness . . ." Kenny, *Philosophical Letters*, 137.

CHAPTER EIGHT: The Certainties of Space and Death

p. 98, "That a vacuum . . ." René Descartes, *Principles of Philosophy* (Boston: D. Reidel, 1983), 46-47.

p. 100, "[E]ach thing, as far as . . ." Ibid., 59.

p. 103, "[A] man, seated . . ." Descartes, *Principles of Philosophy*, 50.

p. 103, "if he turns his attention . . ." Ibid.

CHAPTER NINE: Shoulders of a Giant

p. 117, "If I have seen further . . ." Sir Isaac Newton, *The Correspondence of Isaac Newton,* ed. H. W. Turnbull (Cambridge, UK: Cambridge University Press, 1959), 416.

Bibliography

Alexander, H. G. *The Leibniz-Clarke Correspondence.* Manchester, UK: Manchester University Press, 1956.

Aristotle. *Physics.* Lincoln: University of Nebraska Press, 1961.

Bell, E. T. *Men of Mathematics.* New York: Simon and Schuster, 1937.

Clarke, Desmond. *Descartes: A Biography.* Cambridge, UK: Cambridge University Press, 2006.

Descartes, René. *Compendium of Music (Compendium Musicae).* Translated by Walter Robert. Middleton, WI: American Institute of Musicology, 1961.

———. *Discourse on Method and Meditations on First Philosophy.* Translated by Donald A. Cress. 4th ed. Indianapolis: Hackett, 1998.

———. *Principles of Philosophy.* Translated by Valentine Rodger Miller and Reese P. Miller. Boston: D. Reidel, 1983.

———. *Selected Philosophical Writings.* Edited by John Cottingham, Robert Stoothoff, and Dugald Murdoch. Cambridge, UK: Cambridge University Press, 1988.

Euclid. *Elements.* Cambridge, UK: Cambridge University Press, 1926.

Höffding, Harald. *A History of Modern Philosophy*. New York: Dover, 1955.

Kenny, Anthony, ed. *Descartes: Philosophical Letters*. Minneapolis: University of Minnesota Press, 1970.

Kramer, Edna. *The Nature and Growth of Modern Mathematics*. Princeton, NJ: Princeton University Press, 1970.

Lear, Jonathan. *Aristotle: The Desire to Understand*. Cambridge, UK: Cambridge University Press, 1988.

Mason, Stephen. *A History of the Sciences*. New York: Macmillan: 1956.

Matthews, Michael. *The Scientific Background to Modern Philosophy*. Indianapolis: Hackett, 1989.

Newton, Isaac. *Principia*. Berkeley: University of California Press, 1934.

———. *The Correspondence of Isaac Newton*. Edited by H. W. Turnbull. Cambridge, UK: Cambridge University Press, 1959.

Web sites

http://plato.stanford.edu/contents.html
The Stanford Encyclopedia of Philosophy is an online reference with articles by professional philosophers covering a wide range of topics in every area of philosophy.

http://www-groups.dcs.st-and.ac.uk/~history/
MacTutor History of Mathematics Archive is an extensive collection of essays about mathematical topics and short biographies of a wide range of mathematicians throughout history.

http:// http://www.iep.utm.edu
The Internet Encyclopedia of Philosophy is dedicated to the figures and questions of philosophy.

Glossary

Algebra
The mathematical study of equations.

Analytic geometry
The mathematical study of geometric objects using equations.

Animal spirits
The invisible fluid that Descartes believed flowed through the body in order to cause movement in the muscles and transmit information about observations from the body to the mind.

Copernican
Relating to the view, put forward by the Polish astronomer Nicolaus Copernicus, that the sun is at the center of the universe and that the earth and other planets revolve around it.

Epistemology
The branch of philosophy that examines the nature of human knowledge.

Euclidean geometry
The system of geometric results about figures drawn on a plane surface; also, the systematic treatment of those results by Euclid in his book *Elements*.

Profiles in Mathematics

Inquisition
An institution of the Roman Catholic Church that was charged with rooting out and punishing heretics.

Mechanics
The scientific study of objects in motion.

Metaphysics
The part of philosophy that examines the ultimate nature of reality.

Optics
The scientific study of light.

Index

Aquinas, Saint Thomas, 19, *19*, 21
Aristotle, 19, *20*, 21, 36-37, 57-58, 65, 67, 69-70, 100-101, 104, 110
Ausonius, 48

Bacon, Sir Francis, 54-55, *54*
Balzac, Jean Louis Guez de, 87, *88*
Beeckman, Isaac, 38, 40-41, 43, 52, 67-68
Brouchard, René (uncle), 28

Chandoux, Sieur de, 57-59
Charlet, Father Etienne, 18-19, 104
Christina, Queen of Sweden, 105, *106*
Copernicus, Nicolaus, 37-38, *37*, 73, 97

Descartes, Jeanne (mother), 15-16, 30
Descartes, Joachim (father), 15-17, 28-29, 51
Descartes, Pierre (brother), 15, 28
Descartes, René, *12, 22, 39,* *53, 60, 64, 78, 106, 107*
  Birth, 15
  Birth of daughter, 77
  Death, 107
  Death of daughter, 77
  Publishes first book, *Discourse on Method . . .*, 78
  Publishes *The Principles of Philosophy*, 98
  Works,
    Compendium Musicae, 40-41
    Discourse on the Method for Conducting One's Reason Well and for Seeking Truth in the Sciences, 78, 79, 87
    Le Monde (The World), 68-69, 73-74, 113
    Meditations on First Philosophy, 78, 81
    Olympica, 46
    The Principles of Philosophy, 98, 104-105
    Rules for Guiding One's Intelligence in Searching for the Truth, 55

127

Profiles in Mathematics

Elizabeth, Princess of
   Bohemia, 94-96, 105
Euclid, 13-14, *14*, 19, 24-26,
   38, 53, 114

Fermat, Pierre de, 88, *89*

Galilei, Galileo, 73-74, *73*,
   76, 97, 102-103

Hardy, Claude, 53
Huygens, Christian, 112

Jans, Francine (daughter),
   77, *78*
Jans, Helena, 77

Kant, Immanuel, 110
Kepler, Johannes, 38

Leibniz, Gottfried Wilhelm
   von, 111-114, *111*, 116-117

Martin of Tours, 43, *44*, 45
Maurice, Prince of Orange,
   34-36, *35*, 38, 42, 92-94
Maximilian I, 42-43, 49
Mersenne, Marin, *30*, 31-33,
   52, 65, 67-68, 73-75,
   88, 112
Mydorge, Claude, 56

Newton, Isaac, 112, *112*,
   114-117

Plato, 19, 110
Ptolemy, 36-37, 70

Regius, Henri, 91, 92, 94,
   104-105
Reneri, Henri, 90-91

Viète, François, 88, *90*
Voetius, Gisbertus, 91-92

Wittgenstein, Ludwig, 110